FOREWORD

In 1977 when I wrote my book on *Son Of Sam: The 44-Caliber Killer*, I had said: "Sure it was all in the newspapers. So was Pearl Harbor and World War II and so many other widely-chronicalled events. But they still write books about them. That's what history's about and that's what this book is—a history of a crazed gunman who turned New York into a terror-stricken city for more than a year."

With one exception, that statement holds true in every sense for this book, too. The difference is the killer in the story that follows this page did not spread his terror for a year. Nor a month, a week, or a day. Not even an hour. He ended John Lennon's life in the mere few seconds it took Mark David Chapman to trigger five .38-caliber bullets from a Charter Arms snub-nosed revolver. But in that short span of time, this killer caused more grief and misery and precipitated world-wide mourning as perhaps no assassination before it has.

This book was put together very quickly to serve as a memorial to John Lennon for his fans. Much thought, considerable work, and attention to detail was given, despite the pressure of deadline. I sincerely believe the reader will find much information about John, the Beatles, and about the crime that they did not read in the newspapers and news weeklies, or heard on radio or television.

George Carpozi Jr.

OTHER BOOKS BY
GEORGE CARPOZI JR.

The Brigitte Bardot Story
Marilyn Monroe: Her Own Story
Clark Gable
Let's Twist
Vince Edwards
Red Spies In The U.N.
Red Spies In Washington
Red Spies In The U.S.
Chicago Nurse Murders
The Hidden Side of Jackie Kennedy
Ari & Jackie: For Love Or Money?
The Gary Cooper Story
The Bobby Sherman Story
Three Picassos Before Breakfast
Ordeal By Trial: The Alice Crimmins Story
The Story of John Wayne
The Cop Team
Bugsy Siegel
Cher
The Carol Burnett Story
Always Kill A Brother
The Velvet Jungle
Sunstrike
Son of Sam: The .44-Caliber Killer
Bing Crosby
Man Of Peace: Anwar Sadat
That's Hollywood (A Series: Nos. 1, 2, 3, 4, 5, 6, 7, with others to come)
Crimes Of The Century (A Series: Nos. 1, 2, 3, 4, 5, 6, 7, 8, 9, 10, 11, 12, with others to come)
Frank Sinatra: Is This Man Mafia?

(Mr. Carpozi is presently writing the story of famed horsetrainer Howard (Buddy) Jcobson who was involved in New York's sensational love-triangle murder case.)

JOHN LENNON

DEATH OF A DREAM

George Carpozi Jr.

MANOR
BOOKS
INC.

Bless you for your tears and prayers.
I saw John smiling in the sky.
I saw sorrow changing into clarity.
I saw all of us becoming one mind.
Thank you.

Love, Yoko.

(The blessings John Lennon's widow gave to the millions around the world who kept a silent vigil in his honor from 2 to 2:10 p.m. on Sunday December 14, 1980.)

A MANOR BOOK 1980

Manor Books, Inc.
45 East 30th Street
New York, N.Y. 10016

Published by arrangement with the author.
Printed in the United States.

ISBN: 0-532-23466-9

CONTENTS

BOOK I

A HEINOUS CRIME

I

THE GENTLE BEATLE

He was called "THE GENTLE BEATLE" and "THE THINKING MAN'S BEATLE." John Lennon merited both descriptions through a lifetime of demonstrated sensitivity, insight, courage, and boldness he imparted not only in the music he wrote, but in the everyday conduct of his personal and public demeanor.

His death, a "stupid tragedy," as it was called by the *London Standard,* took a very huge and deeply personal significance to millions of people around the world. Not his fans alone grieved over his senseless yet premeditated murder. Those who had known about Lennon and The Beatles only peripherally—if such a condition could have existed in the face of all the fame and adulation the singing group shared over the nearly two decades of their prominence—also joined in mourning his death.

In the time since The Beatles made their first impact on the music world, at least a dozen singers have died tragically, from Buddy Holly, who was killed in a plane crash in 1959, to John Bonham, the Led Zeppelin who choked on his own vomit after a drinking orgy. In the years between, the Rolling Stones' Brian Jones was drowned; Jimmy Hendrix, Janis Joplin, Elvis Presley, and Keith Moon overdosed on drugs or succumbed to excessive alcohol; the Allman Brothers' Duane Allman and Berry Oakley were killed in motorcycle accidents; Marc Bolan died in an auto crash, and Phil Ochs hanged himself. Only Jim Morrison of The Doors, died a natural death—heart failure.

When John Lennon was shot to death in cold blood that Monday night of December 8, 1980, it was rock'n'roll's first assassination. It also marked not only the loss of an adulated voice, but what many millions felt was the ending of a phase in their own existences.

After the assassin, 25-year-old Mark David Chapman's smoking revolver had stilled the beloved Beatle's life, a shocked, stunned citizenry, so appalled and overwhelmed by the horrendous act of violence, was swift to make comparisons to the similarly brutal killings of President John F. Kennedy, Senator Robert F. Kennedy, and the Rev. Martin Luther King.

There were many in the cities and towns of America and abroad who resented placing the death of a singer in the same category as that of a political or church leader. Yet others around the world, not all rock fans by any means, expressed deep sorrow over Lennon's killing and participated in the various acts of mourning. They demonstrated that the life of this fallen idol warranted bearing grief in their hearts for him as they had done for the other great public figures after their early deaths.

What Lennon's death does have in common with the assassinations of the Kennedys and Rev. King is the feeling of utter despair and helplessness each of these acts inflicts on all people. His wanton killing dramatized anew the seemingly never-ending conflict between the malignancy of terrorism and violence and the search for impossible dreams.

His death stirred the noblest instincts of love and fellowship in peoples at a time when those qualities are submerged in the tensions and madnesses of our times. The sentiment and remembrance transcended all generations, yet those feelings were strongest in those who were growing up in the turbulent 1960s, when the cry to give peace a chance echoed through the world—but went largely ignored.

John Lennon had stunned the musical world in the Summer of 1980 by announcing his comeback after a five-year hiatus as a "house-husband." He had given up his musical career to devote all his time to his 47-year-old wife, Yoko Ono, and their 5-year-old son, Sean. He had lingered in relative anonymity for those five years, which could conceivably have been his most lucrative as a composer and singer. But there were no earthly riches to covet, no mountains to climb for greater glory. John Lennon, at age thirty-five, had it all, a fortune that would amount to an estimated $30 million and fame that few other musical performers had ever enjoyed.

Lennon took his leave from his professional pursuits simply because of his love of family and a desperate desire to avoid becoming a rock'n'roll casualty. In the five years of retirement, he straightened himself out, realigned new goals for himself and for Yoko, and when he was convinced that there was no way he'd fall victim to the danger he dreaded, he emerged from his self-imposed exile.

His first effort, recording a fourteen-song album, *Double Fantasy*, which included the voice of his wife for the first time, had just been issued. More recordings were under way. Then the awful explosion of bullets in the night ended it all.

At forty years of age, John Lennon's life was tragically curtailed. Was it any wonder that this symbol of gentleness and grace precipitated such an outpouring of grief and anguish from so many?

Before his death, Lennon had given a number of interviews—to reporters for *Playboy* magazine, the *RKO Radio Network,* and the *British Broadcasting Company,* among others. Threaded throughout each encounter with his questioners, John leaned toward musing on death and the unknown.

"We're either going to live or we're going to die," he told the *Playboy* reporting team. "If we're dead, we're going to have to deal with that; if we're alive, we're going to have to deal with being alive. So worrying about whether Wall Street, or the Apocalypse is going to come in the form of the great beast...is not going to do us any good day to day."

How ironic that a short time after he had spoken those words, he should be gunned down—at the very moment he felt it was safe to return to the world and give it another helping of his great music which once marched to antiwar rallies and to other causes generated by social consciousness.

Lennon's devotion to causes was almost his undoing. Perhaps no words of his, spoken to those several interviewers in the recent past, are as significant as those that he, together with Yoko, wrote for their album cover:

"With special thanks to all the people, known and unknown, who helped us stay in America, without whom this album would not have been made."

The *help* he referred to bore on his troubles with the United States Immigration & Naturalization Service, which had instituted deportation proceedings against him in the early 1970s.

Ostensibly, the reason the INS tried to keep Lennon out of the country was his London conviction in 1968 on a minor marijuana possession charge.

While on the surface it appeared that INS was after Lennon's scalp, the truth was subsequently unearthed by columnist Jack Anderson. He discovered that U.S. Senator Strom Thurmond, the South Carolina Republican and then chairman of the powerful, witch-hunting Senate Judiciary Committee, had dashed off a secret memo to Attorney General John Mitchell alleging that Lennon's return to the United States from England was designed to have him join ranks with the Yippies and to disrupt the 1972 Republican National Convention.

In part, the letter read:

"Dear John:

"This appears to me to be an important matter, and I

think it would be well for it to be considered at the highest level...Many headaches might be avoided if appropriate action be taken in time."

The letter was passed on to Mitchell's deputy, Richard Kleindienst, who in turn sounded the alarm to INS Commissioner Ray Farrell.

Although too late to intercept Lennon upon his arrival at Kennedy International Airport in New York, the INS nevertheless challenged Lennon's application to stay in the country.

Four long years of give and take in the courts followed. Then finally the U.S. Court of Appeals closed the books on the case on October 7, 1975, with these profound words:

"We have always found a place for those committed to the spirit of liberty. Lennon's four-year battle to remain in our country is testimony to his faith in this American dream."

It is said that The Beatles showed people the way to new things in life, whether they were political relationships, social relationships, sexual relationships, or whatever. And they were credited with having effected such changes upon people and the world they lived in.

Griel Marcus, of *New West Magazine,* brought the meaning of what changes were wrought by The Beatles into focus:

"Lennon was the one who put an edge in all of this, a sense of doubt, struggle, pain, fear, all the kinds of stuff that any form of popular culture simply has to have to be more than trivial...*Strawberry Fields Forever* and *A Day In The Life* said to me: 'This is the way the world is, look out'...With those two songs, it was all compressed, presented in wonderful metaphors in terms of words and music...and that both changed your idea of what you expected off the radio, and changed your attitude about the popular culture you lived in.

"I can say The Beatles, and John Lennon in particular, made me and the other people who cared about them want more out of life than we ever expected to get."

Lennon had political courage, as witnessed by both his songs and his own outspokenness against the Vietnam War. He also had artistic courage to stand up and say the confict was wrong. He was a radical in those times, but there are many who say the world needed John's voice in protest—both his speaking voice and his singing voice.

In that group of four, comprised of Paul McCartney, George Harrison, and Ringo Starr, only John Lennon was the true visionary. A view in that respect was offered by Robert Christgau, of the *Village Voice:*

"It was John who understood, felt, sensed what might be possible…He was an extremely complex, insecure, and perpetually dissatisfied person, and he exploited all of that. The marriage to Yoko changed that, because it gave him another way to feel whole that was perhaps a little less fruitful culturally, though I suspect more satisfying personally.

"I'm sorry we won't get to see what his personal life would have turned out like, as I'm sorry we won't get to see what his artistic life would have turned out like. They would have been an interesting couple to have around at forty-five, at fifty, at seventy…"

No, we shall not see this couple at forty-five, at fifty, nor at seventy. We'll not see them even through forty. For the bullets that the crazed assassin fired into John Lennon's body, into this gentle, thinking man's Beatle, brought the death of a dream…

II
THE MAN BEHIND THE GUN

To Mark David Chapman, life was a tangled, confused landscape upon which he traveled in the guise of many people.

To himself, to others he was a Jekyll-Hyde personality, capable one moment of being charming and compassionate, then frigid, mean-tempered, and even cruel the next.

In the aftermath of John Lennon's assassination, the courts committed Chapman to the care of psychiatrists for thirty days of examinations to determine whether he had the capacity to understand the charges against him and mount his defense at a trial for the Beatle's murder.

Whether the doctors will ever penetrate the dark recesses of Chapman's mind and determine what motivated him to commit this heinous crime is something only time will tell. If there is a rationale to be found for that act, one must not overlook by any means his background and upbringing. Perhaps in that past the alienists may find the spark that ignited the fuse which brought this enigmatical young man six-thousand miles from Honolulu to New York to perform an unspeakable horror on one of the world's greatest entertainment figures.

Mark David Chapman was born May 10, 1955, in Fort Worth, Texas. His father was David Curtis Chapman, originally from Connecticut, and his mother, the former Diane Elizabeth Pease, a native of Massachusetts. The father served with the Air Force at Carswell Air Force Base near Fort Worth, then later worked in an oil company credit department. His mother was a housewife, remaining at home to care for Mark David and a younger sister, Susan.

Mrs. Chapman was described as a strict discipli narian whose heavy hand was perfectly justified after the family moved to Atlanta, Georgia, and Mark David grew into a roisterous, drug-using young teenager.

The Chapmans moved into a typically middle- income white frame-and-brick house in northeast- ern Atlanta. The father also took employment as a loan collector for the Citizens and Southern National Bank.

When he began attending Columbia High School in the Atlanta suburb of Decatur, Mark David became a marked problem child.

"His mother hollered at Mark a lot," said Tammy Morris, a high school friend. "His mother constantly accused him of taking drugs and she spent a lot of time searching his room and putting him on restriction."

He was fourteen when matters got out of hand and Mark David ran away from home. No one can explain the sudden change that came over this once quiet, well-behaved, responsible young man. The Rev. Walter Newton Hendrix Jr., a Baptist minister, went to Columbia High with Chapman and had a distinct recollection of the inexplicable mutation in Mark David's personality and deportment between the eighth and tenth grades.

"My first impression of Mark as an eighth grader was that he was a pretty straight fellow with short hair," Rev. Hendrix remembered. "By the time he reached the tenth grade, he had started wearing his hair long and wearing things like Army jackets."

Garry Limuti, another high school friend, said he could understand that Mark's mother came down hard on him.

"She was justified. Mark had several bad drug experiences," Limuti recalled.

In 1970, Mark vanished into the wind. He was gone, according to friends and associates, a brief while. "No more than two or three months," said one. "But he returned a born-again Christian."

Mr. Hendrix, the minister, had a distinct recollection of Mark in his last two years of high school, after returning from running away.

"He had become deeply attached to Christianity those last two years. He carried a Bible and a 'Jesus notebook.' Mark wasn't wild but he had that hood look about the ninth or tenth grade."

Other former students who went to high school with young Chapman described him as a "Jesus freak."

"He wore a large cross around his neck and quoted scriptures constantly," a former classmate said.

If any hobby fascinated Mark David, none held a candle to his interest and involvement with music. He had an enormous rock'n'roll collection, topped overwhelmingly by The Beatles records—and of those there were many John Lennon singles that were cut between the breakup of the group in 1970 and the singer's 1975 retirement.

In his junior and senior years, while acting out the role of "Jesus freak," Chapman began to moderate his fetish for long hairdos. He had joined a rock band and played the guitar by now—and his appearance was deliberately altered to appear like John Lennon's. Mark combed his hair in Beatle fashion, across his forehead, and wore thin metal-rimmed glasses ala John Lennon.

When he posed for his yearbook picture, Mark appeared before the camera as a round-faced, clear-skinned young man with modishly long, well-groomed hair that resembled The Beatle look.

After graduation in 1973, Chapman enrolled at DeKalb County Junior College. At the same time he pursued an act of social service that he'd undertaken to perform after he became a born-again Christian. His own muddled, unsavory encounter with drugs as a youth brought him to the doorstep of the Young Men's Christian Association.

He volunteered his services as a counseler. He worked

with other young men in the dregs with drugs and he was admired for his effectiveness as their counselor. He also worked for six months in 1975 at a camp for Vietnamese refugees run by the YMCA at Fort Chaffee, Arkansas.

"He was one of the most compassionate, sensitive young people I've ever met," said David C. Moore, director of the YMCA's unit at the refugee camp.

The YMCA assigned Chapman there to perform his services after he had spent a brief while in Lebanon in relief work during the country's civil war. He returned very depressed and, in fact, brought with him a tape recording of gunfire in that war-torn nation.

While at Fort Chaffee, which YMCA officials thought would be a more beneficial locale to do his volunteer work, Chapman played the tape of the gunfire.

"He was also listening constantly to Beatles records," recalled a friend and fellow worker at the camp in Arkansas. "Mark was a very capable person but he dwelled too much on his failings rather than his successes. He was extremely emphatic, but he couldn't get it together."

His effort to squeeze a colleged education between all that other activity was a failure. Mark quit after only a semester at DeKalb Junior College. Yet his pursuit of a higher education went on at a later time—after Lebanon.

It was at Fort Chaffee that Chapman met a young woman, Jessica Blankenship, a pretty, dark-haired eighteen-year-old. The year was 1973. Mark David and Jessica had a three-year relationship during which time she played a significant role in his rehabilitation.

She persuaded him to give up all drugs completely, to abide a religious reawakening (they had met at a prayer meeting just when Chapman took an early interest in Christ and his teachings).

Jessica even got him to enroll with her at Covenant College, a Presbyterian school of higher learning in Lookout Mountain, Tennessee. A few months was all he endured of it. He flunked out and shortly afterward the young woman also turned her back on Mark.

The broken love affair caused him to suffer a mental breakdown.

The Georgia Secretary of State and his staff were unaware of Mark David's mental state in July, 1975, when he filed an application for a security guard's permit, nor did they have any clue to his mental status in July, 1976, when Chapman applied for work as a security guard.

To receive certification for that employment, Chapman took a training course that included firing on a pistol range. Chapman passed the pistol-firing test and received his permit to be a security guard on October 19, 1976. He was then permitted to carry any caliber weapon up to a .38 pistol or 12-gauge shotgun.

He worked briefly as a security guard, first for one firm, then for another. But he wasn't happy in Atlanta. The breakup with Jessica was the last straw. He packed his belongings into two suitcases and once again left the mainland again. This time he took the westward treck all the way to the 50th State. He didn't seem to benefit from the change in scenery. His state of depression persisted and Mark David tried to end it all by inhaling the carbon monoxide fumes from his auto's exhaust. But the suicide try fell short of its mark. The tube running from the exhaust through the window apparently dropped off the tail pipe and by then the twenty-two year old had second thoughts about dying. He was institutionalized briefly after the suicide attempt at Castle Memorial Hospital.

Later that same year, Mark's mother and father visited their son in Honolulu and spent what Mr. Chapman recalls was "a splendid Hawaiian vacation." Mark David was not the disoriented, unhappy young man he was when he was trying to find himself in his teens.

But the father refused to grant that Mark was troublesome as a child or when in his teens. He said his son never showed serious signs of being troubled.

"No, no—once in a great while. But who isn't, once in a while. I just think the buildup came in the last three years. Being unemployed may have depressed him, may have acted on his mind."

Of course, David Chapman was offering that observation after his son was arrested for John Lennon's assassination.

What was the *buildup* Mark David's father spoke of "in the *last three years*"?

The senior Chapman couldn't answer that question. "It's just like a different person than I used to know," he said about his son after he was labelled a killer. "At home, Mark was industrious, cheerful, likeable."

When he and Mrs. Chapman visited Mark in 1977 in Honolulu, "Everything was just super...He took us all over the island..."

But not long after the Chapman's returned to Atlanta, they divorced.

"I've remarried," Chapman said during an interview with a reporter after the crime, "and set up a new life. And he (meaning Mark David) set up his new life when he got married."

The elder Chapman was referring to Mark David's marriage in 1979, to Gloria H. Abe, a 1978 graduate of Kailua High School. The marital vows were taken the following June 2nd in Trinity Presbyterian Church. At the time of the wedding, the bride, who is of Japanese descent, worked in a Honolulu travel agency.

Although she was receiving a handsome income from that business, Chapman pressured her into taking a job in Castle Memorial Hospital's accounting department to be near him. Mark had taken a job in the hospital's print shop in August, 1977, and remained in that employ until November, 1979, when he quit the hospital and took employment as a security guard.

"He made a lot of friends," said Paul Tharp,

community relations director of Castle Memorial. His comment came after the Lennon tragedy. Tharp commented further:

"That's why it surprised me when I heard about (the crime). Mark told us he wanted to work in a job above ground because he liked to be in contact with people."

The marriage was not altogether made in heaven. Besides putting the squeeze on Gloria to switch jobs, he dominated her life in other deplorable ways. He bullied her, forced her to withdraw from an active social life she once enjoyed, and ordered her not to read newspapers or to watch television.

His new employment, with Freeman Guards, Inc. was a stroke of inordinate convenience. He was assigned as a $4-an-hour unarmed guard at the Church of Scientology, directly across the street from his $425-a-month condominium apartment in the Diamond Head Tower, a high rise building at 55 South Kukui Street in downtown Honolulu.

The newlyweds moved into that apartment when they were married. Previously, Mark had lived, from the time of his arrival in Honolulu to his wedding day, in Kailua, a bedroom community on a beach twenty miles from Honolulu, on the opposite side of Oahu.

Sometime after his parents divorced, Mrs. Chapman came to stay on Oahu and is said to have figured prominently in financing her son's trip to his ill-fated encounter with John Lennon. Sources in Honolulu reported she lent Mark $2500.

At the time of that loan, Mark no longer worked for Freeman Guards, an employment that had not been looked upon with favor by other guards on that job.

"He was an extremely nervous type," said one guard. "I don't know why he was ever hired. On a job like we have, you need your cool all the time. That guy didn't have cool."

A member of the Church of Scientology had a more

abusive view of Chapman:

"He was a kook, an absolute nutsy. He shouted abuses at the congregants and staff of the church. He made threatening phone calls and shouted into the mouthpiece: 'Bang! Bang! You're dead!' "

Was Mark David Chapman at this crossroad of his life beginning to crack up?

A definitive answer—if it can ever be arrived at— must await the conclusion of the in-depth psychiatric profile that was begun at Rikers Island Prison in the swiftly-currented waters of the East River off the Bronx shore.

But some insights can be gleaned from Chapman's conduct that may suggest he was beginning to come apart at the seams.

Certainly his behavior as an unarmed guard at the Church of Scientology suggests that.

Chapman also spent hours playing Beatles records loudly in a friend's apartment, as well as his own.

In this period, however incongruous it may seem beside the portrait of his "strangeness," Mark David appeared to have abided an interest in art.

"He became an afficionado of fine art works," said Bob Connell, manager of the condominium complex where Mark and Gloria lived. "He was fond of paintings and stuff like that. He recently bought a popular print of Salvador Dali's version of a Lincoln portrait."

He also showed an appreciation—or at least a fondness for Norman Rockwell's.

Prints weren't all that Mark David Chapman bought while he resided on Oahu...

In mid-October, Chapman walked into the Honolulu police station and filled out an application for a pistol permit.

What reason did he give for wanting to pack a gun?

According to the application, Chapman claimed his apartment had been burglarized in August. Whether the police had a record of a report of that burglary couldn't be determined. Nor does it say anywhere that authorities made any effort to determine the state of Mark David's mental health—his fits of depression, his attempted suicide, and his threatening actions at the church he was supposed to guard.

All that mattered to the authorities issuing the pistol permit was that Chapman didn't have a police record.

On October 23rd, Mark David quit his job as a guard. Prophetically, he signed the employee log book "John Lennon," then crossed it out and signed his name.

Three days later, the Honolulu Police Depart ment issued to Mark David Chapman that piece of paper which authorized him to pack a rod, or as the Constitution phrases it:

"A well-regulated militia, being necessary to the security of a free State, the right of the people to keep and bear arms, shall not be infringed."

When the gun lobbyists make their pilgrimages to Washington and state capitals to oppose weapons-control legislation, they are never without a copy of the Second Amendment to back their claim that the Constitution guarantees them the right to bear arms, such as pistols, rifles, or any other such deadly weapons. The gun lobbies are incensed that states and municipalities have enacted laws against carrying concealed arms without duly authorized licenses.

"Under the Second Amendment, we have the absolute right to bear arms," contends John Adkins, one of the most outspoken of all advocates against weapons control and chief lobbying agent for the 1.8 million-member National Rifle Association.

Actor Jack Lord, who plays the hard-nosed Lieutenant McGarrett in TV's long-running Hawaii 5-O series, apparently wasn't on duty when the 25-year-old Chapman applied at the stationhouse in downtown Honolulu for that pistol permit.

Had Lord been asked to issue the license, he might not

have been as hasty as those authorities were in granting Chapman the right to tote a firearm. Lieutenant McGarrett may have uncovered Mark David's history of mental instability and denied him that "right."

Chapman received the permit on October 23rd. Four days later, he walked into J & S Enterprises— Guns, Honolulu, and looked over their sundry lines of handguns.

As he entered the store, which is a block from police headquarters, Chapman passed the prominently-displayed sign the gun store has installed on its facade:

SUPPORT THE 2nd AMENDMENT...
THE RIGHT TO KEEP AND BEAR ARMS!
BUY A GUN AND GET A BANG OUT OF LIFE!

Mark David made his selection in J & S of a .38-caliber, five-shot Charter Arms revolver with a two- inch barrel. This weapon was the same make of gun that felled Alabama ex-Governor George M. Wallace and paralyzed him from the waist down when the assassin's bullet entered his spine.

This company—Charter Arms Corporation, which manufactures its instruments of death in Bridgeport, Connecticut—had the audacity after the Wallace shooting to file a formal complaint and demand an apology from the Columbia Broadcast ing Company because a television reporter referred to Charter's five-shot revolver used in that crime as "a cheap handgun," an allusion to the "Saturday Night Special" that can be bought for just a few dollars, as compared with the $169 Chapman shelled out for his Charter .38. In cash.

Incredibly, CBS bowed to the demand and apologized to the gun company. In fact, the network groveled and bootlicked Charter, an act that infuriated journalists all over the country (More about this in COMMENTARY Chapter).

Nine days after he purchased the pistol, Chapmen went to the airport in Honolulu and boarded a jetliner with a roundtrip ticket whose return date was December 18.

Before he left wife Gloria, Mark David said:

"I'm going to New York to make it all different..."

III
"I'M SHOT!"

The metal detector at the airport in Honolulu didn't beep with alarm when Mark David Chapman moved his 6-foot, 185-pound frame through its gates. The detector wasn't designed to single out a copy of J.D. Salinger's *Catcher In The Rye,* a wallet, or other innocent items the murder-bent passenger had in his pockets.

The Charter Arms 5-shot .38 caliber snub-nosed revolver was securely out of range of the metal- sniffing detective. Chapman had packed the gun and bullets in his suitcase which was stowed in the belly of the 747 passenger jetliner.

The plane put down at Kennedy Airport on November 7th but we don't have a clear picture of Chapman's itinerary in the city until a month later, the afternoon of Saturday, December 8th, when he returned from a lengthy stay in Decatur and Atlanta, where he visited friends.

He landed at Kennedy again and hailed a taxi that took him to the West Side YMCA on 63rd Street just west of Central Park West. This locale is just nine blocks south of the filigreed wrought iron entry gate to the imposing and historic Dakota apartment building, on Central Park West and 72nd Street, where John Lennon lived with his wife, Yoko Ono, and their son, Shawn.

At the YMCA, Chapman registered under his proper name and paid for a three-night lodging in a $16.60 room. He gave his correct Honolulu address—55 South Kukui Street.

After depositing his suitcase in the room, he came downstairs, walked to Eighth Avenue and West 54th Street and hailed a taxi driver by Mark Snyder.

The 30-year-old cabbie from Brooklyn remembered the ride after recognizing Chapman's face in the newspapers as the passenger he picked up at about 7 p.m. that Saturday.

"He had a package...a brown paper-wrapped package...He told me it contained Beatle tapes... Now thinking back, it might have been a gun..."

His passenger directed Snyder to stop at 62nd Street and Central Park West.

"He left the cab for five minutes. When he came back he started acting weird. He asked me to turn the courtesy light on in the cab and started shuffling papers. He told me he wanted to go to 65th and First. But around Second Avenue, he said, 'This is the stop.' But it was like it didn't make any difference to him what building it was. He went into a building. He came back to the cab two minutes later.

"When he came back he was at a very high energy level. He said, 'Do you listen to rock'n'roll?' I said yeah. He said, 'Well, I got to tell you something because I can't keep this to myself.' He said, 'I got to blurt this out. John Lennon and Paul McCartney just recorded an album and I was the engineer. Mick Jagger was there. I was the engineer for the Rolling Stones, and I was their engineer for 10 years.'"

Chapman also offered him some cocaine before getting out at Bleecker Street and Sixth Avenue.

Next day, he picked up stakes at the "Y" and carried his suitcase with the gun inside it to the stylish Sheraton Centre Hotel at 52nd Street and Seventh Avenue, eleven blocks downtown from the YMCA, twenty blocks from the Dakota or an even mile.

Rooms at the Sheraton start at $70. Chapman had been there the night before and announced his intention to a desk clerk to stay three nights in an $82-a-day room. He paid in cash. Again he used his real name and address.

He didn't require the aid of a bellhop to carry his suitcase up to Room 2730 in the 50-story hotel. That Sunday night, Chapman ordered dinner through room service and ate in his room. The $15 charge was billed to his account.

During the day, Mark David had been noticed hanging around the courtyard of the Dakota apartments—just as he'd been observed loitering there for part of Saturday afternoon and evening. It is not uncommon for celebrity-seekers to stand near the brown-stone, Gothic-designed arched entryway to the courtyard, asking autographs from such residents as Roberta Flack, Leonard Bernstein, Ruth Ford, Lauren Bacall, Gilda Radner, and the Lennons.

The Dakota, in fact, has been used by the entertainment world many times to show class, elegance, and posh living. *Rosemary's Baby* was the most recent vehicle to use the Dakota as backdrop for a movie scenario.

If Chapman had hopes of encountering John Lennon that weekend, he was in for a disappointment. There was no sign of the popular Beatle on Saturday and Sunday.

Chapman was not discouraged. He returned to Central Park West shortly after noon Monday. He encountered free-lance photographer Paul Goresh, loaded down with cameras and picture-taking paraphernalia.

"You waiting to catch Lennon?" asked Chapman.

"Yeah. Where are you from?"

"Hawaii."

"How's it you have a Southern accent?"

"Come from Georgia originally."

"Where you staying now?"

The question caused Chapman's face to cloud.

"Why you wanna know?"

Goresh shrugged and stepped away. Chapman apparently thought the better of his response and came over to the photographer again.

"I wanna apologize I didn't mean to insult you."

"I couldn't care less," Goresh snapped with disdain plain in his voice.

29

"You know," rationalized Chapman, "you can't be too careful these days."

The wait continues. Chapman and Goresh exchange dialogue now and then. Finally around 4:30 o'clock a black man walked by accompanied by a white woman.

"I have no use for them," he said about a salt and pepper couple. "Where I come from, they couldn't get away with that."

All at once it was 5 p.m. and out of the Dakota's entrance came the man that Mark David Chapman had flown 6000 miles to encounter. In his hand, Chapman was holding a recent album. The cover had a background photo of the front of the Dakota apartments, and standing in front of the building were John and Yoko. It was a copy of John's first group of recordings since his retirement in 1965. This was the album entitled *Double Fantasy* in which his 48-year-old Japanese-born wife also sings.

Lennon was accompanied by his wife. They were on their way to the Record Plant studio on West 44th Street to supervise the transfer of some of the album's songs into singles records. Although the album had been out only a month, its sales had already topped 770,000.

The Lennons had lived in the fashionable building all during the 1970s. They first occupied a sunny seventh-floor apartment overlooking Central Park. In recent times, they went through the process of bidding on vacant apartments in the cooperative and were now the proud owners of five of them—a total of twenty-five rooms.

Lennon, dressed in blue denim trousers and black leather jacket over a red shirt, reached the arched entranceway of the Dakota with Yoko on his arm. Little Sean had been left behind upstairs with the nursemaid. At the curb, his sleek Cadillac limousine was waiting with the chauffeur behind the wheel.

"Mr. Lennon...Mr. Lennon," called out the tall stranger with a deeply tanned face that gave his blue eyes an added cerulean glow. "I just bought your new album. I am wild about it. Please...please...will you autograph it for me? Please...?"

"Sure, let me have it," Lennon said. He took the album and scribbled his signature across the face of it. Photographer Paul Goresh clicked away. He had gotten more than he'd expected. The long encampment outside the Dakota for the Beatle's photo had paid off handsomely. Not only did the lensman catch John and Yoko together, but he was able to frame an interesting composition with a "fan" having the Lennon's best-selling album autographed by *The Man* himself.

"Thank you, Mr. Lennon. Thank you so much..." the stranger said, backing away with a slight bow.

John and Ono got into their limousine and were driven away. The time was five minutes past 5 o'clock.

Mark David Chapman looked at the album with seeming pride. But that lasted for a brief few moments. He then walked to the doorman's brass booth to the left of the entrance and placed the album down.

He walked back to the photographer, who was changing film and preparing for another celebrity to emerge or enter the Dakota.

"Did I have my hat on or off in the picture?" he asked.

The answer was inconclusive. "I don't remember."

"Damn, I wanted it off. Oh, wow...they'll never believe this in Hawaii."

Goresh kept his vigil at the Dakota until 7:45 p.m.

"I think I'll call it quits," the photographer told Chapman. Goresh still knew virtually nothing about this apparently eccentric stranger who staked out the Dakota to get John Lennon's autograph, and still hung out for two-and-a-half hours more for no apparent reason.

"Hey, man," Chapman implored. "Don't go. Stick it out. Stick around. You never know..."

"What do you mean?"

"Something might happen. You know, he could go to

Spain or something tonight and you might never see him again."

"I'm not worried about that," snapped Goresh. "I've put in a long day. So long..."

Mark David Chapman remained for the vigil that only he knew its purpose...

Three days before this Monday, December 8th, John Lennon had sat in a cozy Manhattan restaurant with his wife and a British interviewer. He was talking about life in his adopted city of New York.

"Here," Lennon said, "I can go to the movies or restaurants. I have been walking about in the streets for the past seven years. When I left England I couldn't even walk around the block."

The answer was precipitated by the British Broadcasting Company reporter's question about the safety or danger Lennon felt New York City posed. Although Lennon had always been enthusias tic about New York as a home base, many of his friends had tried to persuade John to leave the city.

"His friends believed it was dangerous for John and Yoko to live there," said concert promoter Dirk Summers, who was trying to reunite the Beatles and revive their career as a group.

"Those friends felt something tragic might befall John. They wanted him to move to Los Angeles. They felt John would be safer out there. But John insisted that he wanted to stay in New York."

Of all places that New Yorker's fear—Central Park—John Lennon felt safest. In fact, to promote his new album just before Thanksgiving of 1980, he and Yoko took a stroll through the park for a TV commercial to promote *Double Fantasy*.

John Lennon couldn't have been more pleased about his comeback than on Monday night, December 8th. Until then nothing untoward had ever happened to disenfranchise them from their love affair with the Big Apple. Indeed, that Central Park that lay directly across the street from the Dakota, and so dreaded as a dangerous piece of real estate by so many New Yorkers and visitors, was a favorite place for John and Yoko and little Sean.

Of course, the problem was the deluge of fans who were begging for his autograph or, for the more rowdy and aggressive ones, a piece of his clothing, anything—a souvenir.

Lennon felt especially secure living in the 96-year-old Dakota, which got its name when the Dakota Territory was America's last frontier and the building was New York City's first luxury apartment house—the first tall residential building well north of Manhattan's midtown.

Lennon and Yoko became a neighborhood fixture.

Stacey Lindeman, a songwriter residing on West 74th Street, often saw the Lennons at a fruit and vegetable store on Columbus Avenue and 73rd Street.

"They looked so ordinary," Miss Lindeman observed. "It was hard to realize that he was John Lennon and she was Yoko. They were so famous. They were just a little family, shopping for something for dinner. I wanted to speak to them but it seemed it would be an imposition."

A doorman, Tim Reid, who worked in a building a half block away, also had a view of the Lennons.

"Sure I used to see them out there, mostly when it was warm. No one bothered them. I mean, there's a lot of famous people around here—especially in the Dakota."

He could have added that beside Leonard Bernstein and the other aforementioned famous personalities, the Dakota numbered among its tenants such renowned public figures as Greta Garbo, Katherine Hepburn, Herbert Hoover, Douglas MacArthur, Richard Nixon, Adlai Steven son, the Shah of Iran's children, Ronald Reagan's son, and Mick Jagger.

John Lennon's total lack of fear about living in New

York was expressed most explicitly on Monday, December 8th—at 10 o'clock in the morning—in an interview taped for future broad- cast by RKO General Radio Network.

In excerpting done by RKO General, a portion— the most significant—of the interview went this way with John Lennon's responses:

We're either going to live or we're going to die. If we're dead we're going to have to deal with that, if we're alive we're going to have to deal with being alive. So worrying about whether Wall Street, or the Apocalypse is going to come in the form of the Great Beast—is not going to do us any good day to day.

•

I'm talking to guys and gals who had been through what we had been through together, the 60's group that has survived—survived the war, the drugs, the politics, the violence on the street, the whole shebang, that we survived it, and we're here and I'm talking to them and the women's song is to Yoko and it's to all women.

The thing the 60's did was show us the possibility and the responsibility that we all had. It wasn't the answer, it just gave us a glimpse of the possibility— and in the 70's everybody's going nah, nah, nah and possibly in the 80's everyone will say, "O.K. let's project the positive side of life again."

•

I don't want to have to sell my soul again, as it were, to have a hit record. I've discovered that I can live without it, and it makes it happier for me.

•

After ten, fifteen, almost twenty years of being under contract, and having to produce two albums a year and a single every three months, in the early days, regardless of what the hell else was doing, or what your family life was like or what your personal life was like, nothing counted, you just had to get those songs up.

•

We feel like this is just a start now, you see, "Double Fantasy"—this is our first album—I know we've worked together before, we've even made albums together before—but this is our first album, we feel, I feel like nothing has ever happened before today.

•

You have to give thanks to God or whatever is up there, the fact that we all survived. We all survived Vietnam or Watergate, the tremendous upheaval of the whole world. It changed. We were the hit ones of the 60's.

But the world is not like the 60's, the whole world's changed. I am going into an unknown future, but I'm still all here. And still, while there's life, there's hope.

John Lennon had barely eleven hours more to live after having spoken those prophetic words about life and death.

But death was his last expectation during the better part of four hours that he and Yoko spent at the Record Plant picking tunes from the album for singles sales.

At about 10:15 p.m., John turned to his producer, Jack Douglas, and said:

"Hey, okay we call it a night? I'm bushed. We'll be back in the morning. Yoko and I want to stop and have a bite to eat on the way home."

"Okay with me," said Douglas. "Have fun, John. Good night, Yoko."

John and his wife then left the studio.

"Although we had planned to stop somewhere and eat," Yoko Ono was to say later, "we decided not to. We went straight home instead. We were going to check on Sean and then go out for a bite..."

Sean had been left in the care of his nursemaid, Helen Seamen, and presumably was asleep by the time his parents were returning to the Dakota, shortly before 11 o'clock.

Neither John nor Yoko could have expected a fan to be waiting in the shadows under the entrance at that late hour for an autograph. The street was nearly deserted. A few people were walking about on that unseasonably warm December night. Temperatures during the day hovered over the sixties. Even now the thermometer was barely below fifty degrees.

John and Yoko alighted from their limousine at the curb and strolled into the archway leading to the Dakota's large courtyard. John was a long stride or two ahead of Yoko.

All at once they were startled by a voice coming from a recess in the courtyard. They turned and saw a man standing in the shadows just inside the arch.

"Mr. Lennon!" he called out.

John and Yoko turned and saw a man standing— the same man who earlier in the evening beseiged the Beatle for his autograph on the record album.

No one can now know what thoughts raced through Lennon's mind at that precise moment. But Yoko's eyes opened wide, her mind froze in horror.

The man had a gun. He was holding it with two hands. Not an instant after he called out John's name, the man crouched into a combat stance and fire spewed from the muzzle of his .38-caliber Charter Arms five-shot revolver. The deadly slugs plowed into John Lennon with unerring accuracy.

He screamed in pain and cried out, "I'm shot!"

"I didn't realize at first that John had been hit," Yoko said the next day. "He kept walking. Then he fell and I saw blood."

Four persons viewed this heinous act: One was a doorman; an elevator operator and a cab driver who had just dropped off a passenger were the others.

John was now clutching his chest and staggering forward toward the Dakota's entrance. He managed to climb six short steps to the room used by the concierge.

"I'm shot!" he repeated. His legs faltered as he gasped those words and he collapsed to the floor.

Yoko ran to her stricken husband's side, crying hysterically. She lifted John's head and cradled it in her arms. Then she screamed to several people who heard the shots and ran up to her.

"Help me!" she pleaded.

Help was on its way...

IV
DEATH OF A BEATLE

The first policemen to respond to a wave of phone calls to the emergency 911 number of the New York City Police Department were Officers Steve Spiro and Peter Cullen, who were patrolling in their blue and white police radio cruiser at Broadway and 72nd Street.

Spiro and Cullen could not assist Lennon because their first observation at the scene commanded their immediate and total attention.

The gunman was standing to the left of the archway. The weapon was not in his hands. After he emptied the gun at John, Mark David Chapman cried out, "That's it!" Then he tossed the snub-nosed revolver into a bush.

The elevator operator, who witnessed the shooting, ran over, picked up the gun, and held it for safekeeping. He turned it over to Officer Spiro, after he and Cullen went through the ritual of spreadeagling the prisoner and patting him down.

When the policemen entered the arch, Chapman already had prepared himself for the arrest. He had both hands on his head, his forearms forward so they partially shielded his face.

"Don't hurt me," he cried out as the cops approached.

"No one's going to hurt you," Cullen said. "Just turn around and place your hands against that wall, your feet apart." Both officers had their service revolvers unholstered and were gripping the butts. But they didn't have to go beyond that step. No force was necessary to take this gunman.

As Cullen patted down the prisoner, he spoke again.

"Don't let anyone hurt me. Stay with me."

"He's clean," Cullen said to his partner, Spiro. "Cuff him, Steve." Neither officer responded to Chapman's plea to not let anyone hurt him.

Spiro clamped the cuffs on Chapman's wrists behind his back.

All that Mark David's pockets yielded in the search were his wallet, keys, and a copy of Salinger's *Catcher In The Rye*. Later, when the contents of the wallet were examined, it was found to contain $2000 in cash.

While . Chapman was being neutralized other policemen from the 20th Precinct stationhouse on West 82nd Street raced to the Dakota.

Arriving virtually on the heels of Spiro and Cullen were Police Officers Bill Gamble and James Moran, who immediately saw that Cullen and Spiro had the situation in hand with the suspect and quickly sensed they were needed at the Dakota's entrance where a man was stretched on the ground and a woman was holding his head in her arms:

As they passed the suspect, Gamble was to recall afterward:

"I heard him say to Pete and Steve, 'I've got a big man inside me and I've got a little man inside of me. The little man is the one who pulled the trigger.' "

Gamble and Moran recognized the gravity of Lennon's wounds the instant they reached his side. He was conscious but the blood was pouring from his body at an alarming flow.

"What is your name?" Gamble asked as he put his arms under the Beatle's back to lift him up. The policeman asked the question only to determine whether or not the victim was conscious.

"I could hear him breathing heavily and I wanted to keep him conscious until we got to the hospital," Gamble explained later. "I could see the holes in his chest and I knew there wasn't any time to waste."

Lennon answered with his given and last name.

"Can't wait an ambulance," Gamble said to Moran. "We've got to take him to the hospital in the car."

Moran then grasped Lennon's legs and Gamble

gripped John by the underarms, cradled them in the crooks of his elbows, and together the policemen carried him to the police car. They settled him on the back seat and Gamble kneeled on the floor to steady the dying man. Moran ran to the driver's side, hit his roof emergency light panel button and tweeters. The police car raced at speeds of more than 50 mph through lightly trafficked streets enroute to the nearest emergency medical facility, Roosevelt Hospital, on West 59th Street, some fourteen blocks away or just a shade more than a half mile.

In the back, Gamble tried to continue the conversation with Lennon to keep him conscious.

"Are you sure you're John Lennon?" asked the policeman.

"I am," the answer came.

"How do you feel?"

"I'm in pain..."

Gamble kept up the effort to converse with Lennon but his voice grew weaker and his breathing shallow.

"He also sounded confused," Gamble remembered afterward.

Moran had radioed an alert to have a rolling stretcher waiting at the entrance of Roosevelt's emergency section. When they arrived—the ride took less than three minutes—doctors and nurses were standing by. Lennon was lifted out of the police car, again by the two policemen and placed on the stretcher, which was then rolled by the hospital staff into the emergency room.

One of the first physicians to minister to the stricken Beatle was Dr. Stephen Lynn, the medical director of the hospital's emergency room.

Dr. Lynn and the other physicians worked desperately over the wounded Lennon, whose breath no longer was labored and weak, as it had been on the desperate ride to the hospital. His breathing had stopped and a paleness was becoming apparent on his face.

"I'm pretty certain he was dead at the time of his

arrival," Dr. Lynn said later. "Yet we weren't prepared to give up on him."

The doctors performed blood transfusions, surgical procedures, and other efforts to revive Lennon so that he could be taken to surgery. But the efforts were in vain. Lennon was pronounced dead by Dr. Lynn at 11:15 p.m.

Although the gunman appeared to have fired all five shots into Lennon's chest, all the bullets did not strike him fully in front.

As we would be told later following an autopsy performed at the city mortuary in the Bellevue Hospital complex by Dr. Elliot M. Gross, the Chief Medical Examiner, four shots struck Lennon, two in the left side of his back and two in his left shoulder.

"All four caused internal damage and bleeding," said Dr. Gross. "I cannot estimate the distance from which they were fired but they must have been from more than eighteen inches because there were no powder burns."

Dr. Gross also said Lennon could not have survived the wounds under any circumstances.

"Mr. Lennon died of shock and loss of blood. No one could have lived more than a few minutes with such injuries..."

Even as Officers Gamble and Moran were speeding the stricken Beatle to Roosevelt Hospital, not far behind them raced another police car, driven by Officer Anthony Palma, who conveyed Yoko Ono to her husband's side in the emergency room.

Yoko was hysterical.

"Tell me it's not true...Tell me...please tell me that it is not true...John is not shot...Please tell me that..."

Palma didn't know what to say to her. He was a true Beatle fan in the 1960s and he was on the verge of tears himself.

At the hospital, Yoko stood by silently watching the valient but futile efforts to bring her husband back to life. She subsequently regained a measure of composure and begged to be allowed to make a phone call.

"I want to call Shawn and tell him what happened to his father," she said.

After the phone call, Yoko learned the bitter truth—that John couldn't be saved. Her distress on hearing this news from Dr. Lynn is indescribable.

Many hours later, she issued a statement through record producer Geffen:

"John loved and prayed for the human race. Please do the same for him..."

When Yoko was escorted back to the Dakota by Geffen and police, a crowd of nearly two-hundred was gathered outside the apartment house. Within the hour, more than six-hundred Beatle fans and curious were assembled outside the apartment building, spilling from the sidewalk into the street.

They were weeping, many of them. Many were chanting. Others were singing. This was the beginning of a vigil that would count millions of Beatles fans in the mass gatherings all over the world in a mourning unprecedented for any entertainment figure in history.

Many of the more macabre of those in the crowd looked past the gray wooden police horses set up in front of the archway to glimpse the chips in the stone caused by the bullets and the blood on the ground that was illuminated by police spotlights beamed by members of the Emergency Service Unit to aid Crime Scene detectives in their search for evidence.

The killer had been removed from the scene long before even the first dozen onlookers had gathered. Police Officers Spiro and Cullen whisked him away in their police car so swiftly because they feared the possibility that the crowds might take matters in their own hands with the slayer.

As he was bundled into the police car for the ride to the 82nd Street police station, Chapman again pleaded for his safety.

"Don't let anybody hurt me..."

On the ride uptown, Mark David blurted, "I didn't have anything against him. I don't know why I did it..."

The words trailed off. Then into another train of thought he went.

"I've always had a lot of respect for the police..."

When dawn broke over New York, the crowd outside the Dakota had not diminished since midnight. If anything, it seemed to have grown. Scores of policemen were on duty now, keeping the people away from the Dakota behind the NYPD's gray-painted wooden horses.

The mourners were mostly in their twenties and thirties and their gathering at the Dakota made it seem as they had come to say goodbye to an era—an era that very few other performers had ever duplicated with the sort of electrical excitement The Beatles created and the adoration they commanded from their fans.

John Lennon was one of four members of a singing group and yet he seemed to rise above the others because of his immense talent and ability to define new areas in music—and define, indeed, a lifestyle that had sustained itself even into the eighties.

His voice was the voice of youth, a voice of freedom bridging the generation gaps. It was a voice that died tragically in the courtyard of the Dakota apartments that Monday night of December 8, 1980.

But John Lennon left his legacy for all the world to have and to hold. His voice was stilled, yet it really wasn't. It has been preserved on records, on TV films and tapes, and in movie footages that shall remain for as many years as any of us and generations to follow, for as long as appreciation remains for John Lennon's monumental contributions not only to the world of music, but to the world as a whole.

V

NEXT DAY

In the early hours of Tuesday, December 10th, when the rising sun was still low in the Eastern horizon, Yoko Ono took Sean by the hand and brought him downstairs.

They walked into the courtyard to a certain spot. Let Yoko tell what came next...

I told Sean what happened. I showed him the picture of his father on the cover of the paper and explained the situation. I took Sean to the spot where John lay after he was shot.

Sean wanted to know why the person shot John if he liked John. I explained that he was probably a confused person. Sean said we should find out if he was confused or if he really meant to kill John.

I said that was up to the court. He asked what court—a tennis court or a basketball court?

That's how Sean used to talk with his father. They were buddies. John would have been proud of Sean if he had heard this.

Sean cried later. He also said, "Now Daddy is part of God. I guess when you die you become much more bigger because you're part of everything."

I don't have much more to add to Sean's statement. The silent vigil will take place December 14th at 2 PM for 10 minutes.

Our thoughts will be with you.

Love, Yoko and Sean

That same morning, from the seclusion of her apartment, Yoko arranged for the cremation of her husband's body at the Ferncliff crematorium in suburban Hartsdale, north of the city in Westchester County.

The arrangements for moving the body from the city mortuary to the crematorium were entrusted to the Frank E. Campbell Funeral Chapel at 1076 Madison Avenue. The body was to be released in early afternoon following the autopsy by the chief medical examiner, Dr. Gross.

But the body would not leave before a paparazzi- type photographer had sneaked into the "cutting room" and taken a picture of John Lennon lying on a slab in the morgue.

The photo was sold to the *New York Post* by an agency named Sygma for an undisclosed sum and was splashed on Page One the morning after with a caption that read:

...AND HERE JOHN LENNON RESTS IN PEACE

● This poignant photo of John Lennon was taken not long before he was moved from the city morgue to Campbell's Funeral Home on Madison Av prior to his cremation—the last journey of a man much loved, a man much grieved, a man dead much before his time.

Dr. Gross was furious when he saw that photo and ordered an immediate investigation to determine who among his staff may have cooperated with the photographer. The city mortuary is patrolled by guards and the entrance has elaborate procedures for keeping out persons who have no business there.

Many days later, Dr. Gross was still at a loss to learn who took the picture and what person or persons in the morgue were in cahoots with the lensman.

New York County District Attorney Robert Morgenthau then launched a grand jury investigation to get to the bottom of the scandal.

Another scandal was in the making in the Dakota courtyard where the Crime Scene Unit was still gathering evidence long after daybreak when the Emergency Service Unit's spotlights were dismantled and removed.

That album—*Double Fantasy*—which Mark David Chapman had placed next to the doorman's brass booth, after he obtained the autograph, which was signed, "John Lennon, 1980," had disappeared!

Apparently some souvenir hunter had snapped it up in the confusion following the shooting.

"We don't have it and we don't know where it is," bemoaned Detective Ronnie Hoffman, the top sleuth on the homicide investigation. "We need it for fingerprints."

The album, of course, would command an astronomical price from a Beatles memorabilia collector. More importantly, however, the investigators wanted it back because it was a vital link in the chain of evidence against Chapman.

"We hope the person who swiped the album will come forward with it," said Hoffman. Then he added ominously between gritted teeth: "Otherwise we'll simply have to track down the culprit. And track him we will..."

There was no need to send the troops out for the album snatcher.

Not many hours after Detective Hoffman had spoken and his words appeared in print, the album reappeared in police hands just as mysteriously as it had disappeared.

"We got it back," said Hoffman. "How isn't important right now. The main thing is that this important piece of evidence is now back in the hands of authorities..."

The joy at the 20th Precinct stationhouse over the return of the album was about the only bright note in an otherwise sad day.

Many persons had gone to bed before the late newscasters on radio and television had clarioned their reports on John Lennon's assassination. Those people, perhaps numbering in the millions in the Eastern time zone, heard it in the morning upon awakening on their radios or TV sets, and were jolted by the news in the screaming headlines of the morning papers.

The sadness that spread worldwide as the news reached even the remotest corners of the Earth caused an incredible, tragic phenomenon in at least two households we know about...

Two Beatles fans committed suicide!

Sixteen-year-old Colleen Costello left a note in her home in Brooksville, Florida, saying she was depressed over Lennon's death. Then she swallowed a fatal overdose of sleeping pills.

"Lennon's death was the straw that broke the camel's back," said her saddened mother, Jean Costello, who found her daughter dead on the floor of her bedroom when she came home for lunch on that Tuesday afternoon.

Mrs. Costello said Colleen had been deeply depressed since her father's suicide in February.

In Salt Lake City, Utah, thirty-year-old Michael Craig shot himself to death in despondency over the Beatle's killing.

Craig, according to witnesses, became upset on learning Lennon had been slain. Seventeen-year-old Lisa Renak told authorities Craig had been discussing John's death when all at once he said: "I think I'll end it all."

He then pulled a pistol from his pocket, stuck the muzzle into his mouth, and pulled the trigger.

Paramedics pronounced him dead at the scene minutes later.

When those deaths were reported by authorities in Brooksville and Salt Lake City, Yoko Ono was deeply disturbed. Despite her own profound anguish, Yoko made a plea to her husband's followers not to surrender to despair or to commit suicide.

In a telephone interview with the New York *Daily News,* Yoko said in an emotion-choked voice:

"It's hard. I wish I could tell you how hard it is. I've told Sean and he's crying. I'm afraid he'll be crying more.

"So many things are happening, and I keep catching myself saying: 'John, look at this.'

"People are committing suicide. They are sending me telegrams saying that this is the end of an era and everything. I'm really so concerned.

"But this is not the end of an era. *Starting Over* still goes." She was referring to John's record with that title. "The eighties are still going to be a beautiful time, and John believed it."

Yoko told the *News* she was afraid people would think of John's death as "the end of something." She went on:

"But it was just starting, and we know that the eighties is up to each one of us and that should not stop.

"That sort of thinking is against what we believe in, and when something like this happens, each one of us must go on."

Yoko reiterated what she had asked in her statement earlier when she described how she showed Sean where his father died. It dwelled on the vigil she had asked Lennon's fans to hold worldwide, saying:

"I'd like John's fans to remember him with ten minutes of silent prayer at two p.m. Sunday because everyone must pray together so that it will be the way John believed in."

Mayor Ed Koch had already announced the mourners could assemble and pray at the bandshell in Central Park, a stone's throw from the Dakota on 72nd Street.

"John loved and prayed for the human race," Yoko said. "Please pray the same for him. Please remember that he had deep faith and concern for life, and though he has now joined the greater force, he is still with us here."

NYPD detectives spread out into other areas of investigation beside the one being conducted at the Dakota.

A team of sleuths led by Detective Sergeant Tom Brady went to both the West Side YMCA on 63rd Street and to the Sheraton Center to check on Mark David Chapman's movements, as well as to unearth any evidence that would give authorities an insight of the killer and his possible motivation in taking Lennon's life so precipitately.

"He came to the city carrying a three-foot-long suitcase," Sergeant Brady said after those areas of the investigation were completed. "It seems Chapman brought along only a couple of changes of underwear and a shaving kit. That's all we found in the suitcase."

The detectives learned that Chapman actually booked rooms for the same night at both hostelries. He had shelled out $49.50 for a three-night lodging in the YMCA and $180 for an overlapping two- night stay at the Sheraton Centre.

On a table in his hotel room suite, Chapman had left a placemat decorated with a tableau from the film *The Wizard of Oz,* depicting Judy Garland in a pose with the Tin Man, the Cowardly Lion, and the Scarecrow, played respectively by Jack Haley, Bert Lahr, and Ray Bolger. Judy was Dorothy in the picture, of course.

At the police station on 82nd Street where Chapman had been taken after his arrest, the scene was bedlam. The second-floor interrogation room, where the prisoner was closeted with detectives and was being questioned, was the only place with a semblance of order. Elsewhere on that floor and downstairs, it was a madhouse with reporters and photographers and cameramen and their equipment everywhere.

Finally a semblance of order came when Chief of

Detectives James Sullivan walke dinto the first- floor muster room and stood before the booking desk.

As cameras whirred and flashguns and strobe lights lit up the place in an ever-exploding blaze of blinding light, Sullivan addressed the assemblage of journalists:

"We have arrested Mark David Chapman, age twenty-five of fifty-five South Kukui Street, Honolulu, Hawaii..."

That launched the killer's identity into orbit— literally. Satellites bounced the name of Mark David Chapman around the globe. Reporters who dashed for the phones in the police station to notify their city desks and radio assignment editors of the assassin's name and address, also triggered heavy action in Honolulu. Reporters and photographers raced pell mell to 55 South Kukui, which is the Diamond Head Tower, and beseiged Chapman's wife Gloria for comment.

In their initial encounter with Mrs. Chapman, reporters did a double-take when they learned that Mark David's wife was of Japanese descent, the same ethnic origin as Yoko Ono.

At first Gloria wouldn't talk with the media, then she relented. Her statement:

"I'm a Christian, and I believe that forgiveness is an important thing. I'm terribly sorry that the killing happened. Being a Beatles fan, I mourn the death of John Lennon. But as a Christian I can forgive my husband..."

Did she want to sent a message to Mark David?

"Yes. 'I love you.' "

The time was 6:20 a.m. and the scene at the West 82nd Street police station had hardly changed. Pandemonium continued, especially this minute when it was decided to transport Chapman to the Manhattan Criminal Court Building to await arraignment on charges of murder and other crimes, including possession of a weapon, etc.

Chapman shuffled out of the stationhouse in

handcuffs, accompanied by a phalanx of uniformed and plainclothes policemen. He was shunted immediately into the back of a police van, whose doors were quickly slammed shut and locked.

Photographers didn't get the shots they had wanted. Mark David came out of the building with his coat over his head.

Downtown on Centre Street, Chapman was taken into the huge courthouse and confined to a third-floor cell, 8 feet by 6 feet small, where at first he paced back and forth and later sat in a corner staring blankly at the wall.

He remained there until shortly after 3 p.m. when he was escorted under heavy guard to Courtroom 129 for arraignment. Chapman's face was expressionless and his hands were riffling sheets of white toilet paper that he was gradually padding into a wad.

Spectators packed the courtroom. Before any were admitted, however, court officers led them through a metal detector to guard against the possibility of another Dallas, or as one detective put it:

"We don't want another Jack Ruby," referring to the stationhouse murder of President John F. Kennedy's assassin Harvey Oswald, by the Dallas nightclub owner.

By this time, an attorney, Herbert J. Adlerberg, a noted criminal lawyer, was appointed by the court to represent Chapman at the proceedings before the bar of justice.

Criminal Court Judge Martin Rettinger was at once confronted with a contentious battery of barristers. Adlerberg clashed right at the start with Assistant District Attorney Kim Hogrefe after she addressed the bench:

"The evidence shows the defendent commited the deliberate, premeditated execution of John Lennon. The defendent had two-thousand dollars on his person for the purpose of coming to New York to do what he has done..."

Adlerberg at once protested:

"My client is psychologically impaired...He has tried to commit suicide twice and might be unfit to stand trial..."

Chapman, surrounded by no fewer than twenty court officers at any time during the five-minute proceedings, remained impassive throughout. His only movement was with his hands, whose fingers kept twirling and compressing the toilet paper.

"I want to ask you a question," Judge Rettinger said to Chapman, who then turned his eyes toward the bench.

"Do you understand your rights as a defendant?"

Chapman did not respond. Nor did he answer when asked to plead to the charges.

His lawyer asked the court to commit his client for a psychiatric examination, which was granted. Adlerberg also asked the judge to order an around-the-clock suicide watch because "my client is not fully cognizant and has twice tried to take his life..."

Over the objections of Prosecutor Hogrefe, Rettinger placed Chapman under a suicide watch in the psychiatric ward at Bellevue Hospital for thirty days of observation.

After Chapman was led away for the ride in a heavily-guarded caravan of Correction Department vehicles to the hospital, Adlerberg spoke with reporters.

"I have to believe Mark Chapman isn't all there. His answers were not connected to my questions in any way..."

The lawyer also disclosed that Chapman had given him a motive and rationale for the murder, but Adlerberg wouldn't say what Mark David had told him.

Adlerberg did reveal that Chapman told him he had tried to kill himself with the same revolver on an earlier visit to New York, which was probably around November 7th or 8th, after arriving in the city from Honolulu.

His whereabout between that time and his presence in New York that was recorded in the registers of the

YMCA and the Sheraton—Saturday, December 8th—wasn't known entirely. Authorities were able to account for only a few days of that month, and they were able to do that by speaking with Jessica Blankenship, his former girlfriend, and her parents, as well as Paul Visscher, a friend in the Atlanta area.

The Blankenships told police that Chapman abruptly showed up at their door the weekend of November 8th. But the parents, aware of Chapman's drug and mental problems from the past, did not allow Jessica, now twenty-five years old, to remain alone with the visitor.

It was not divulged what Chapman spoke about with their daughter, but the visit was brief.

Reports from Atlanta indicated that Chapman had been seen by a number of persons, who said he appeared casual and in control of himself. Some said he had told them he had borrowed $2500 to finance his trip so he could visit his hometown.

Paul Visscher, who hadn't seen Mark David for several years, until his recent visit, said:

"He seemed like he was in good spirits. Others told me, however, that he seemed depressed. But he didn't seem that way to me at all. And he didn't mention John Lennon once."

But in Honolulu, a filmmaker, Kenneth Anger, remembered distinctly an odd encounter he had with Chapman in September—when Mark David referred to Lennon and his wife by their first names.

Anger, who is fifty, was showing a film at the University of Hawaii when he was confronted by Chapman, who asked:

"Oh, you know Mick Jagger, you know Anita Pallenberg, and you know John and Yoko...?"

"He kept bugging me," Anger said. "He went down the list of rock stars I knew."

Just as they were parting, Chapman shook Anger's hand—and gave him two .38-caliber bullets!

"Take these as souvenirs of our conversation," Chapman told the bewildered movie-maker.

Back at the Dakota, Yoko Ono mourned her husband's death in the privacy of her apartment, surrounded by several friends...

One of them, Elliot Mintz, a publicity man based in Los Angeles, described the scene inside the Lennon apartment as "just grim."

Mintz had come downstairs briefly to speak with reporters, and while he did he straightened the flowers and picture of John that the hundreds of fans now gathered outside had placed on the building's front gate. At the same time he collected the notes written by many in the grieving crowd to Yoko, who had asked to read them.

"She is resting. She is distraught. But she won't see her doctor although we have asked her to. She is holding her own and showing a great deal of strength. We are trying to keep her in bed as long as possible and we don't want her to leave the building for at least two days.

"She is determined to find the strength to write a statement to the world which she hopes can adequately reflect her own thoughts and what John would have wanted to say."

By this time, Ringo Starr and his fiancee, actress Barbara Bach, had arrived in his limousine and gone upstairs to join Yoko Ono in her grief.

On the street, hundreds of mourners—at times the number reached nearly a thousand, if not more— withstood a cooling trend in the weather during the day and continued the vigil that had begun just minutes after the news of John Lennon's murder spread the night before.

As night fell, the temperatures dropped but the crowds remained, shivering and shaking tambourines with their trembling hands. Actually the tambourines were accompaniment to the old Beatle ballads the fans were singing.

Of course not all could have been fans of *The Beatles* when they were singing together and setting records everywhere for crowds and followers. It was easy to see that some of the youthful, long-haired, denim-clad men and women maintaining the vigil must have been in diapers in those days. But they were in earnest in their desire to pay tribute to The Beatles, their music, and to the memory of John Lennon as some of the older folks, including mothers and fathers, who were teenagers in the 1960s, as well as grandmothers and grandfathers, who were a lot older in those days but had let themselves to be caught up in the musical magnetism the Liverpudlians spread everywhere they went.

Waitresses from Hisae's Restaurant on 72nd Street at one point during the night carried trays of steaming coffee, donated by the management, to Lennon's shivering fans, most of whom were caught without gloves or umbrellas to shield them against a steady, icy drizzle that started to fall.

A woman apartment dweller in the building across 72nd shouted angrily at the crowd from her window, "Why don't you all just go on home and let Miss Ono mourn in peace?"

Someone in the crowd shouted back:

"We're mourning, too, in case you hadn't noticed."

And that's the way it was on that Tuesday, December 9th, the day after John Lennon's senseless murder...

VI

VIGIL

In midafternoon of Tuesday, December 10th, the second day following his death, John Lennon's body was placed in a mahogany casket at the Frank E. Campbell Funeral Chapel and taken in a hearse to the Ferncliff Crematorium in Hartsdale. The medical examiner had released the remains to the undertaker earlier and it was transported uptown to the chapel in a body bag.

The funeral was in secret to assure Yoko Ono and the handful of family friends the privacy they wanted for the cremation. John's ashes were preserved but there was no public announcement of what was done with them.

Attention at the moment was directed to Bellevue Hospital where Mark David Chapman was being examined to establish his state of mind. Dr. Marvin Stone, a ward doctor, reported:

"The patient seems a little depressed. He would like to know how his family is doing. He has asked about his wife and his mother."

Chapman's Bellevue residency was fated to be a short one. Fearing that Lennon fans might beseige the hospital when they gathered for the Sunday vigil in Central Park, fifty blocks uptown, authorities transferred the prisoner to inaccessible Rikers Island Prison in the East River..

Surrounded by an army of shotgun-carrying policemen, Chapman was whisked from the hospital to the prison infirmary. There he was covered by one of the most elaborate security blankets since David Berkowitz, the Son of Sam, .44-caliber killer, was taken in custody in 1977.

Edward Hirshey, a Correction Department spokesman, said:

"The feeling is that he would be safer on Rikers. For

one thing, there's only one bridge leading to Rikers. Bellevue is in the middle of Manhattan. It's just easier to keep people away from Rikers than from Bellevue."

Hirshey explained that the tests would still be conducted at Bellevue. "We will bus him, under heavy guard of course, whenever he is scheduled for examination and consultation with the doctors at the hospital."

In the midst of the continuing mourning over Lennon's death, the inevitable issue of his estate became a topic of interest. His will, filed for probate in New York County Surrogate's Court by the law firm of Kimmelman, Sexter & Sobel, listed an estate of $30 million, which was left to "my beloved wife" and a trust fund.

The will bequeathed half to Yoko and the other half of the vast estate to a trust fund the Beatle and his wife set up when the will was drawn and signed November 12, 1979. It showed that Lennon owned luxury apartments, a number of mansions, a 62-foot yacht, a twin-engine plane, and by no means least a 25 percent interest of Apple Records, which holds copyrights to the Beatles' music and was still a major source of Lennon's annual income. Each of the four Beatles held a fourth share in the corporation.

The principal eye-opening properties included the five co-op units in the Dakota apartments that were estimated to have a value of $1.5 million, a $700,000 beachfront seven-bedroom home in Palm Beach, Florida, and a $450,000 shorefront home in Cold Spring Harbor on Long Island. Additionally, the Lennons had acquired in recent times several dairy farms in upstate New York communities of Delhi and Oneonta. The eight parcels of farmland were assessed at the time of purchase at a half million dollars, but in the three years since their worth had doubled. Just one of Lennon's 250 prize Holsteins sold in early 1980 for a record $265,000 at the state fair in

Syracuse.

Filing the will wasn't the only action on the legal front. Defense lawyer Herbert Adlerberg appeared in the Criminal Courts Building for a second time as counsel for Mark Chapman, but on this Thursday, December 11, he was there to represent himself rather than his client.

Adlerberg went before Judge Rena K. Uviller and asked to be relieved of his assignment to defend Chapman. The judge promptly did so, replacing him as counsel with another experienced criminal lawyer, Jonathan Marks.

Why did Alderberg ask to be taken off the case?

"I've practiced before the criminal courts here for more than twenty-one years," he explained. "This case, however, has become something of an albatross for me. Because of the notoriety, I have been on the telephone constantly with journalists wanting information about Mr. Chapman and with crank callers offering their help.

"It would be detrimental to the defendant if I remained on this case."

Judge Uviller granted the request immediately. Then outside court, Alderberg tried to put reports to rest that his life had been threatened.

"That's not true. What's happened in the past few days has been beyond any proportion I believed it would be. I've handled many cases before, the black Liberation Army and the Harlem Six, but this is in a class by itself. I can't handle it. It is too much."

Chapman's new lawyer, Marks, was a 37-year-old graduate of Harvard Law School, who worked for four years in the United States Attorney's office in Brooklyn before entering private practice.

John Lennon's death triggered a wave of commercialism that, if it had not exceeded, at least equaled, the race of the mass merchandisers, movie moguls, book publishers, and various entertainment industry entrepreneurs who capitalized on Elvis Presley's death.

Some 200 million Elvis records were sold worldwide in the four months following Presley's death. It was too soon to tell how many John Lennon and Beatles records would be sold, but many of those who "feed on the dead" predicted the figure might be double, perhaps even three times larger.

The rush to market "Lennon-abilia" took several directions.

A tiny Delaware firm, Factors, Etc., which claimed exclusive marketing rights to Elvis Presley memorabilia and souvenirs, contacted Lennon's record label and family lawyers to obtain licensing agreements to market T-shirt transfers, posters, belt buckles, and other items with John's name and/or face.

United Artists hastily rebooked such Beatles films as *Let It Be, Yellow Submarine,* and *How I Won The War* for release to movie theaters worldwide. Those titles were also being prepared for release on videotape for home viewing.

The producers of *Beatlemania,* the theatrical recreation of The Beatles music planned to tour the country with more companies to play to the largest number of live audiences possible.

The merchandisers saw dollar signs dancing before their eyes everywhere as they raced to capitalize on the slain Beatle.

Sunday, December 14th, dawned and the crowds had already begun to gather in Central Park for the 2 p.m. ten-minute vigil to Lennon's memory that Yoko had requested.

Although police had estimated the throngs could reach as many as 500,000, the actual number was closer to 100,000. But the scene was repeated around the nation and the world. Boston, Los Angeles, Philadelphia,

Seattle, Salt Lake City, Toledo, Miami, and literally hundreds of other cities, villages, and hamlets in the United States, Canada, and elsewhere took part in this unprecedented tribute to a singer.

The mourners came to Central Park with flowers in their hair. Others brought flaming candles. Many wore commemorative T-shirts and buttons. A goodly number carried transistor radios and tape recorders that played Beatle music. And some even carried banners and pictures of John.

It was a chilly day, the sky was mostly overcast, reflecting the sombre mood of the crowd, but the warmth in the people's hearts for The Gentle Beatle was in evidence everywhere in this crowd that massed on the mall and the field in front of the Central Park band shell, where a larger-than-life photo of the slain singer graced the stage on its easel, surrounded by flowers and wreaths.

This was by far the largest vigil anywhere.

Promptly at 2 p.m. the crowd was asked to begin the ten-minute period of silence. And promptly they did. The hush that fell over the huge assemblage was deafening. The ABC-TV network, which broadcast an entire hour-long program of the vigil and film clips of Lennon and the Beatles in song, also observed the memorial without a word for the ten minutes from anchorman Roger Grimsby or other reporters who covered the event in Central Park.

The vigils were not without their moments of violence.

In Central Park, a 19-year-old youth in the crowd was shot in the chest when he tackled a man menacing a group of people with a pistol.

The vigil in Liverpool erupted into chaos when thousands of distraught fans, apparently angered when a rock band switched to playing non-Beatles music, swarmed onto a makeshift stage. The stage collapsed and about 100 persons were injured.

Not all persons took to the vigil with approbation.

At 2 p.m. when the vigil began, cashier Suzanne Stephens, a 17-year-old employed in a store in Long Island's Lake Ronkonkoma, bowed her head. A customer waiting to pay, walked out. Another was irritated because Suzanne wouldn't take a payment for purchases.

The manager came over and when Suzanne persisted in maintaining her silence till the end of the vigil, she was promptly fired.

"I believe that the vigil was important," said an unrepentant Suzanne.

From New York's Albany, the state capital, another discordant note was sounded by Senator Richard E. Schermerhorn, an arch conservative from Newburgh who was elected to office on the Republican and Conservative Party lines.

"I am baffled by the page after page of newspaper stories glorifying a man who wrote songs in the sixties that were drug-related and encouraged the use of drugs by our young people.

"He was, in my opinion, a leader of the hippie movement and encouraged the deterioration of the young. He wrote songs that were anti-religion, anti-God, and anti-American. He was one of the leaders of marchers to Washington against this country and its involvement in the Vietnam War, while thousands of men were giving their lives to maintain peace throughout the world."

Schermerhorn said the praise heaped on Lennon more properly belonged to former New York Yankees catcher Elston Howard, who died over the weekend at the age of fifty-one. Howard was the first black to play for the Bronx Bombers and also the first American League player to win the Most Valuable Player Award.

Schermerhorn said when the Legislature returned to Albany in the new year, he would introduce a resolution honoring Howard and ask to adjourn the day's session in the ballplayer's honor.

"If such a resolution is introduced for John Lennon," he threatened, "I will speak against it and vote against it."

The Senator pointed a finger at the news media. "The press has made a hero out of someone who was a champion in the drug movement, a champion in un-American demonstrations and slogans, who should have never been allowed in the country again after his first drug arrest."

Beatle fans and others who agree or do not agree with Schermerhorn's stand, may write to the Senator at Lakeside Plaza, Newburgh, N.Y. 12550, or phone him at (914) 561-2102.

The last word after the vigil came from Yoko Ono when she sent blessings to the hundreds of thousands, if not millions, who kept the silent vigil around the world that memorable Sunday. Her five-line note read:

> *Bless you for your tears and prayers.*
> *I saw John smiling in the sky.*
> *I saw sorrow changing into clarity.*
> *I saw all of us becoming one mind.*
> *Thank you.*
>
> *Love, Yoko*

BOOK II

HIS LEGACY

VII

BIRTH OF THE BEATLES

In their order of birth, Ringo Starr was the first Beatle to open his eyes on this planet. He was born Richard Starkey on July 7, 1940, at 9 Madryn Street in the rough and tumble Dingle section of Liverpool, England.

His parents, Richard Starkey and the former Elsie Gleave, were married in 1936 while both were working in a bakery. They were living in a rented six-room house when Ringo was born, and soon afterward German bombers dropped their lethal cargoes on Liverpool in the first air raid of the city following the outbreak of World War II.

Richie, as Ringo was called then, has no recollection of the bombings. By the time he was old enough to know a war was going on, the Allies had the Germans on the run and the skies over Great Britain were swept clean of Nazi planes.

When John Winston Lennon made his debut in Oxford Street Maternity Hospital in Liverpool, his birth came in the middle of an air raid. His parents, Fred Lennon and the former Julia Stanley, had married December 3, 1938, but their conjugal union did not endure. In fact, neither did Ringo's mother and father remain married for long after he was born. Ringo was only three when his parents went their separate ways, and he remained with his mother.

However, mother and baby were forced to live in a less expensive rented house at 10 Admiral Grove, around the corner from the place Ringo was born. This residence had only two rooms up and two down.

John Winston Lennon—years later he'd change his middle name to Ono in honor of his wife—was given an option at the age of five to live either with his mother or father after their split. Greatly torn between the two, he made the difficult decision of staying with his mother.

But that was of short duration. He eventually went to live with his Aunt Mimi, one of Mrs. Lennon's four sisters. John was taken to Aunt Mimi's and husband George's house at 251 Menlove Avenue, Woolton, Liverpool, where he lived for many years as the couple raised him as their own son.

Aunt Mimi played the greatest influence on John Lennon's life as well as in the formation of the Beatles. For after little John grew up from a boy with unruly hair, a snappish tongue, and a penchant for poetry which he read and wrote as well, he brought his friends to the house to rehearse—and the friends were Paul McCartney and George Harrison (Ringo was not yet part of the group that John was trying to form).

At first Aunt Mimi had the greatest apprehension about admitting John's seedy-looking friends into the house. They had long hair, unpressed shirts, and battered jeans. This was not the sort of company John's aunt wanted him to keep. After all, she brought him up in adolescence with neatly pressed short-pants suits, clean shirts, and always made certain he had that scrubbed look about him.

But John's glibness overcame Aunt Mimi's objections. At a later time, he'd outtalk his aunt about her desire to have him study art at Liverpool University.

John showed talents for art at an early age. They didn't exactly lock him in his room to sketch and paint, but his aunt and uncle made it a rule that he had to spend several hours a day at the easel. And he did. But he wasn't always painting.

He was secretly composing poetry those times!

Through life, John Lennon maintained a cynical front because of two of the most traumatic childhood experiences any youngster can experience.

His father, who was a porter, actually abandoned his

wife and joined the British Navy. The divorce came after he returned. Mrs. Lennon wanted to raise her son herself, but was too poor to care for him properly.

John remained close to his mother but was much closer to Aunt Mimi. Julia Stanley Lennon died in Liverpool in 1957, while John was attending high school. She was fatally injured by an automobile.

As good a student as John had been in grammar school, he was unable to maintain his high scholarship in high school. Mainly because from the time John was fifteen years old he was bitten by the musical bug. The more he devoted himself to music—he composed lyrics and words—the more his class grades dropped off.

Even before his sixteenth birthday—the year was 1955—Lennon organized his first rock and roll group, the Quarrymen. The influencing forces that led John to his tremendous interest in music were Elvis Presley, Little Richard, and Jerry Lee Lewis—the earliest American rock and roll stars.

John adopted the name for his group from the Quarry Bank High School he was attending. None of the other members of the future group to be known as The Beatles were Quarrymen then.

James Paul McCartney was born June 18, 1942, in Liverpool's Walton Hospital. His arrival was in high style, occurring in a private ward. This was not because his family was so well-to-do—they were working-class people. But his mother had been the head nurse in the maternity ward and her former colleagues were determined to give her special attention when she was delivered of her first-born.

Paul's parents, Jim McCartney and the former Mary Patricia Mohin, also had a second son, Michael. When Paul was fourteen years old, his mother died. His father then raised the boys.

Immediately after his mother's death, Paul bought a

guitar and began playing it. The time is not too far off when Paul and his guitar will have a fateful rendezvous with other aspiring young musicians, who will do much in revolutionizing rock 'n' roll as the world then knew it.

George Harrison was born February 25, 1943, at 12 Arnold Grove in Liverpool's Wavetree section. Like Paul, he was a first-born son. His parents were Harold Harrison and the former Louise French, who married May 20, 1930.

George also had a sister, Louise, and two brothers, Harold and Peter. He also had the most normal or conventional childhood of The Beatles.

George attended the same school in Liverpool, Dovedale Primary, as John had. Although their paths undoubtedly had crossed, they never met there formally. George was nearly three years younger, so he was in a lower grade then John. But it's said that George's older brother, Peter, and John were acquainted in school because both were in the same class.

In 1954, George transferred to the Liverpool Institute, attended by Paul as well, one grade ahead of young Harrison.

George's musical inclinations began after his thirteenth birthday in 1956 when he bought a guitar from a schoolmate for three pounds—less than $10 in U.S. currency then. George played the guitar until he had mastered its chords and decided he had to graduate to an electric model.

His mother plunked down the forty-five pounds— $150—for the instrument and George Harrison was on his way to fulfilling destiny's plan that a great rock 'n' roll group shall be formed one day soon.

George soon mastered the electric guitar and he formed a group with some friendsd called The Rebels. They were given an audition at the Speke British Legion Club. The Speke section of Liverpool is where the

Harrisons were living then, at 25 Upton Green.

The Rebels played all of one night at the club and were rewarded with the modest sum of ten shillings.

John Lennon's group, The Quarrymen, made their debut on June 15, 1956, at the Woolton Parish Church festival in Liverpool, with John playing lead guitar.

A friend of Lennon's from school, Ivan Vaughan, brought along another friend to see The Quarrymen's performance. The friend Vaughan introduced to John Lennon was Paul McCartney.

John was sixteen years old and Paul fourteen then. And if they had not been introduced to each other, the likelihood of their meeting another time would seem remote. And just as distant, it might seem, that The Beatles would have come into existence as we know them.

Paul, though younger, was a much more accomplished musician at that stage in their careers. After watching The Quarrymen perform, Paul gave them pointers on playing the guitar. In future times he would claim credit for having taught John to play new chords on the guitar that day.

Paul played some himself, too. He showed John how to do a popular song of the era, *Twenty Flight Rock*. John was impressed greatly. He wanted to have Paul join The Quarrymen. But one thing disturbed Lennon.

"If I bring him in, will it affect my status as leader of the group?" John asked himself. But Lennon had considerable confidence in himself and decided Paul couldn't undermine his dominance of the group even though he was bringing a greater measure of musical knowledge into the Quarrymen than Lennon was then capable of contributing.

John soon began being influenced by Paul, who was writing his own songs. So John started writing his own songs as well.

In 1958 Paul introduced John to one of his friends from the Liverpool Institute—George Harrison.

Again fate took matters in hand. George listened to The Quarrymen's performance in Wilson Hall in Garston. Paul introduced him to John, who remarked that if George could play the guitar as well as Eddie Clayton, who was on the same bill that night with another group, then George was welcome to join The Quarrymen.

George accepted the challenge by tearing off a quick rendition of *Raunchy*. That won him a spot with The Quarrymen.

The previous influence of skiffle—and English-type music which relied on washboards and tea chests as substitute instruments—suddenly gave way to a new rock sound from the United States.

It was 1956 and Elvis Presley had burst upon the scene worldwide. His style, his music, and his widespread acceptance and success could not be ignored by any musical group.

Although The Quarrymen did lean to the new rock sounds from across the Atlantic, and despite the budding young talents of John, Paul, and George, The Quarrymen didn't make it. They disbanded in November, 1959.

George became an apprentice electrician in a Liverpool department store, Blackers. Initially, he'd been sent there by an employment agency to work as a window dresser.

John and Paul didn't do much of anything in the way of earning a livelihood until 1960 when they, together with George, formed a new musical group, Johnny and The Moondogs. They were granted an audition for Carroll Levis' television program and were booked for one telecast that was to be done in Manchester.

But the show ran late and the boys had to leave before the final number—the time audience applause is measured—to catch the last train home to Liverpool. No one can say what impact Johnny and The Moondogs might have made on the audience or whether John, Paul and George might have been launched on successful careers had they not had to leave.

Another audition loomed for the group later that same year. Larry Parnes, one of the giants of British rock 'n' roll at that time, had such biggies in his stable of recording artists as Tommy Steele, Bill Fury, and Johnny Gentle.

When the trio heard impresario Parnes was coming to Liverpool in a talent search, John, Paul, and George arranged to audition for him at the Blue Angel Club.

They had decided to do away with the name Johnny and The Moondogs because it didn't sound professional. So when the time neared for their tryout they were nameless.

It was John Lennon who came up with an identity for the group. He'd been impressed with the successful American group called Buddy Holly and The Crickets. He decided another insect name might be appropriate. He suggested The Beatles. Someone else suggested Long John and The Silver Beatles.

By audition time at the Blue Angel, the boys had shortened the name to Silver Beatles.

A friend of Lennon's from school, Ivan Vaughan, brought along another friend to see The Quarrymen's performance. The friend Vaughan introduced to John Lennon was Paul McCartney.

John was sixteen years old and Paul fourteen then. And if they had not been introduced to each other, the likelihood of their meeting another time would seem remote. And just as distant, it might seem, that The Beatles would have come into existence as we know them.

Paul, though younger, was a much more accomplished musician at that stage in their careers. After watching The Quarrymen perform, Paul gave them pointers on playing the guitar. In future times he would claim credit for having taught John to play new chords on the guitar that day.

Paul played some himself, too. He showed John how

to do a popular song of the era, *Twenty Flight Rock*. John was impressed greatly. He wanted to have Paul join The Quarrymen. But one thing disturbed Lennon.

"If I bring him in, will it affect my status as leader of the group?" John asked himself. But Lennon had considerable confidence in himself and decided Paul couldn't undermine his dominance of the group even though he was bringing a greater measure of musical knowledge into the Quarrymen than Lennon was then capable of contributing.

John soon began being influenced by Paul, who was writing his own songs. So John started writing his own songs as well.

In 1958 Paul introduced John to one of his friends from the Liverpool Institute—George Harrison.

Again fate took matters in hand. George listened to The Quarrymen's performance in Wilson Hall in Garston. Paul introduced him to John, who remarked that if George could play the guitar as well as Eddie Clayton, who was on the same bill that night with another group, then George was welcome to join The Quarrymen.

George accepted the challenge by tearing off a quick rendition of *Raunchy*. That won him a spot with The Quarrymen.

The previous influence of skiffle—and English-type music which relied on washboards and tea chests as substitute instruments—suddenly gave way to a new rock sound from the United States.

It was 1956 and Elvis Presley had burst upon the scene worldwide. His style, his music, and his widespread acceptance and success could not be ignored by any musical group.

Although The Quarrymen did lean to the new rock sounds from across the Atlantic, and despite the budding young talents of John, Paul, and George, The Quarrymen didn't make it. They disbanded in November, 1959.

George became an apprentice electrician in a Liverpool department store, Blackers. Initially, he'd been sent there by an employment agency to work as a window dresser.

John and Paul didn't do much of anything in the way of earning a livelihood until 1960 when they, together with George, formed a new musical group, Johnny and The Moondogs. They were granted an audition for Carroll Levis' television program and were booked for one telecast that was to be done in Manchester.

But the show ran late and the boys had to leave before the final number—the time audience applause is measured—to catch the last train home to Liverpool. No one can say what impact Johnny and The Moondogs might have made on the audience or whether John, Paul and George might have been launched on successful careers had they not had to leave.

Another audition loomed for the group later that same year. Larry Parnes, one of the giants of British rock 'n' roll at that time, had such biggies in his stable of recording artists as Tommy Steele, Bill Fury, and Johnny Gentle.

When the trio heard impresario Parnes was coming to Liverpool in a talent search, John, Paul, and George arranged to audition for him at the Blue Angel Club.

They had decided to do away with the name Johnny and The Moondogs because it didn't sound professional. So when the time neared for their tryout they were nameless.

It was John Lennon who came up with an identity for the group. He'd been impressed with the successful American group called Buddy Holly and The Crickets. He decided another insect name might be appropriate. He suggested The Beatles. Someone else suggested Long John and The Silver Beatles.

By audition time at the Blue Angel, the boys had shortened the name to Silver Beatles.

Things went well for the group now. They were hired.

But instead of being the back-up band for Bill Fury, they were sent on a two-week tour of Scotland with Johnny Gentle. For that trip they adopted new stage names—Carl Harrison for George, a great admirer of the American singer Carl Perkins, Paul Ramon for Paul, and Johnny Silver for John.

The bass guitar was an indispensible instrument for the group and the player on that instrument was a fourth Silver Beatle named Stu Sutcliffe. Like the others, Sutcliffe, a friend of John's from school, had not yet acquired professional polish. But, somehow, the group played well together despite their lack of experience.

Their tour of Scotland over, the Silver Beatles returned to Liverpool where they worked an engagement in a strip club. Later they performed at a nightclub where they were destined to rocket to fame at a future time. The place was the Cavern Club on Mathew Street. Their services at their first engagement there were remunerated with a small amount of pounds.

When guitarist Ken Brown departed, the Silver Beatles took on a drummer named Pete Best. Pete's mother was then operating the Casbah Club in Liverpool, where the old Quarrymen had played with some success. But the Casbah wouldn't get the Silver Beatles now.

Their success in Scotland opened an opportunity to place their talents on a stage in Hamburg, West Germany, whose population then was double that of Liverpool. They were signed to play eight hours a night at the Indra Club at a stipend that could hardly be called a king's ransom—not when it was fifteen pounds a week, or $45.

In October, 1960, authorities shuttered the Indra Club because of the noise it generated. The Silver Beatles then moved to another Hamburg night spot, the Kaiserkeller. It was there that the boys began popping diet pills to stay alert for their grueling nights on the bandstand, where they alternated for six hours during every evening's performance with another Liverpool group, Rory Storme and The Hurricanes.

Back home, The Hurricanes were a much better-known
group than the Silver Beatles. Their drummer was none other than Ringo Starr!

Suddenly bad things began happening for the Silver Beatles. In December, 1960, George Harrison was deported by the German authorities for being underage and not possessing resident or work permits. The others were forced to leave Hamburg after Paul and Pete Best were arrested for accidentally starting a fire in a nightclub. They came home to Liverpool in low spirits.

But their fortunes underwent another change. On December 27, 1960, the Silver Beatles appeared in Liverpool at Litherland Town Hall. They were a smash. They became the talk of the town. Their experiences in Hamburg had helped put them over the top in Liverpool.

The Silver Beatles new hard rock sound contrasted greatly with the more typical Cliff Richard sound of English pop music at the time.

At Litherland, they were billed simply as "The Beatles, Direct From Hamburg." The engagement came about through the efforts of Bob Wooler, a disc jockey at Liverpool's Cavern Club and an early Beatle's enthusiast. He was responsible for getting their booking into the Cavern Club in January, 1961. The Cavern's 8 Mathew Street address has since become one of the most famous in the world. Ironically, today it no longer exists.

In April, 1961, The Beatles, as they were now known, returned to Hamburg. George was now old enough—18 years—not to be denied a visa and license to work because he was no longer a minor.

The Beatles appeared at the Top Ten Club, where they played from 7 p.m. to 2 a.m., except Saturdays when they were on stage until 3 a.m.

During this second tour of Hamburg, The Beatles made their first recordings. They were signed by German recording executive and orchestra leader Bert Kaempfert to back singer Tony Sheridan. They were billed on the records as The Beat Brothers. In those days, the world wasn't accustomed to recording groups by such oddball names as The Beatles.

But The Beatles had been born. First, they'd come into this world through their mother's wombs, each in his own turn and time—first, Ringo, then John, followed by Paul and George.

Then they were born as The Beatles in Liverpool's Litherland Town Hall.

The Beatles!

A name of a singing group destined to go down in musical history!

VIII
TO THE TOP OF THE CHARTS

In July, 1961, John, Paul, George and Pete Best returned to Liverpool. By now, Stu Sutcliffe had left The Beatles. He had been unable to live with the other Beatles, who were always picking on him. Stu, who'd been an art student, stayed on in Hamburg and enrolled in an art school there.

In July 1961 John, Paul, George and Pete Best returned to Liverpool. Their first show on returning was done with another group that had been kicking around Liverpool for a long time, Gerry and The Pacemakers.

The Beatles' popularity continued in Liverpool, and the Cavern Club became their nightclub home.

The Cavern was physically not far from a record store in Whitechapel Street called Nems which stood for North End Music Stores. It was here, on October 29, 1961, that a youngster named Raymond Jones was to start the ball rolling in the direction of Beatlemania by requesting a recording called *My Bonnie* by a group called The Beatles.

The proprietor of the shop, Brian Epstein, had to confess that he had no idea who The Beatles were and did not have any record by them in stock.

On November 9, 1961 Brian Epstein did some personal research on this new group called The Beatles. He visited the Cavern Club during a noontime session and was impressed with The Beatles and the response of the audience to them. He wound up ordering some 200 copies of *My Bonnie* from the German record company Deutsche Gramophone, which had released it on the Polydor label. Brian visited the Cavern Club on several other occasions, and in turn asked The Beatles to come to his office for a talk on December 3, 1961. Shortly thereafter Brian Epstein became the manager of The Beatles, with a signed contract giving him 25 percent of their earnings. He formed a new company, Nems Enterprises, to handle management of The Beatles.

Having been in the business of selling records, Brian Epstein had some knowledge of the British recording industry. He used his contacts to arrange an audition for The Beatles at Decca Records in London on January 1, 1926. George did a rendition of *The Sheik of Araby,* and Paul performed *Red Sails In The Sunset* and *Like Dreamers Do.*

At first it appeared that things had gone well, but ultimately Decca decided against signing The Beatles. Instead, they picked up Brian Poole & The Tremeloes. Brian Epstein warned Decca that The Beatles would someday be bigger than Elvis Presley.

In April, 1962, Stu Sutcliffe died in Hamburg of a brain hemorrhage. The same month The Beatles returned to Hamburg and opened at the new Star Club. Brian had refused to book them back into the Top Ten Club, which had offered them about one-third less money than the Star came up with. When The Beatles turned the Top Ten Club down, it was unable to come up with a back-up group for singer Tony Sheridan. But a drummer named Ringo Starr was hired to back him up. So, once again, Ringo's path crossed The Beatles.

The Beatles returned to England in early June 1962. They had an audition, arranged by Brian Epstein, with George Martin at the studios of EMI/Parlophone Records in St. John's Wood, London on June 6, 1962.

Nothing definite came out of it, and they returned to Liverpool where they opened at the Cavern Club on June 9. Epstein had booked them into various situations throughout the summer.

In late July The Beatles' biggest break to that time came. George Martin revealed that he would sign them to a contract with Parlophone. But as things were going to turn out it would not be John, Paul, George, and Pete who would record for Parlophone.

By mid-August, Pete Best was fired from the group.

To this day no one really knows exactly why The Beatles decided to drop Pete. It's been rumored that George really was the one who wanted him out of the group.

But that's been denied by the other Beatles, who have said they decided amongst themselves to drop Pete. Brian Epstein had the unpleasant job of giving him the bad news.

George Martin has suggested that his own unhappiness with Pete's drumming may have precipitated the Beatles' action. But the truth is, nobody knows for certain.

Pete happened to have been one of the most popular Beatles, and when he was fired his supporters picketed the Cavern Club and even went so far as to attack the other members of the group!

To replace Pete Best, of course, The Beatles turned to Ringo Starr. Ringo had been working in Hamburg with Rory Storme & The Hurricanes. They had returned to Liverpool, and then Ringo had gone back to Hamburg to back-up Tony Sheridan.

Now he was going to work with Rory Storme once again. At the same time that The Beatles offered him a spot as their drummer, another group called King Size Taylor & The Dominoes asked Ringo to come on board. Reportedly, The Beatles were willing to pay him about five pounds a week more so he decided to tie in with them.

On August 23, 1962, John married Cynthia Powell, his girlfriend for quite some time, at the Mount Pleasant Register Office in Liverpool.

Although they tried very hard to keep the news of their marriage from coming out, it did. Their biggest fear had been that the fans would no longer like John now that he was married.

That, of course, proved not to be the case.

On September 11, 1962 George Martin scheduled The Beatles to record their first British record. It featured *Love Me Do* on the "A" side and *P.S. I Love You* on the "B" or flip side. A studio musician named Andy White had been hired by George Martin to play the drums during this recording session.

In view of The Beatles' problems with the drums in the past and in view of George Martin's uncertainty about Ringo's skill on the drums, he had decided to play it safe and bring in an expert. When. *P.S. I Love You* was first recorded, Ringo was only playing the maracas.

Happily for Ringo, another version of the same record was recorded afterwards on which he was given an opportunity to play the drums himself. In so doing he proved himself and was never again taken off drums for a Beatles recording session.

The group's first record was released in England on October 4, 1962. *Love Me Do* ultimately got up to Number 17 on the British music charts. A record they turned down, *How Do You Do It,* was recorded instead by Gerry & The Pacemakers.

It hit the Number One spot on the charts.

The Beatles recorded their second single, *Please Please Me* on November 26, 1962. It was released on January 12, 1963 and became the Number One record in England on February 16, 1963. It was The Beatles' first top record.

The Beatles closed out 1962 by returning to Hamburg in December for their fifth and, as things turned out, final tour.

They began 1963 with a tour of Scotland in January. The following month they made their first national tour of Britain with the Helen Shapiro Show. They were billed after Helen Shapiro, Danny Williams, and Kenny Lunch; but were ahead of the Kestrels and the Red Price Orchestra.

Another milestone for The Beatles was their

appearance in February on the *Thank Your Lucky Stars* television show. It was the first time they'd ever been on TV.

In March 1963 The Beatles were touring again, this time with Chris Montez and Tommy Roe as the stars of the show. But The Beatles were no longer unknowns. They were getting their own following now.

On April 8, 1963 John and Cynthia Lennon's son, Julian, was born at Sefton General Hospital in Liverpool.

Three days later The Beatles' single *From Me To You* was released in England. April also saw the release of The Beatles' first LP, *Please Please Me,* in the United Kingdom. It became a Number One album.

The Beatles toured again in May and June, but this time they were the headliners. Also on the bill were Gerry & The Pacemakers and Roy Orbison. Shortly afterwards Paul turned 21.

In Liverpool again, The Beatles performed at the Cavern Club. Their last appearance there was on August 23, 1963. A few months later The Beatles were to hit the big time.

October 13, 1963, is the day that Beatlemania arrived in England. Prior to this The Beatles were new and somewhat successful group with a strong following in Liverpool.

But Liverpool was not London, and London was where the action in the entertainment world really was centered.

On the 13th of October, 1963 The Beatles were appearing as the stars of the television program *Sunday Night At the London Palladium,* which was telecast throughout Great Britain on the ATV network.

Some 15 million viewers were estimated to have watched them on television that night. What looked like millions of fans crowded the streets outside the

Palladium to get a glimpse of The Beatles in person!

From October 24-29 The Beatles toured Sweden, and appeared on television there. They were now becoming an international phenomenon, too. They returned to London for an appearance on November 4 at the Royal Variety Performance at the Prince of Wales Theatre.

In addition to the audience in the theatre, some 26 million people throughout Great Britain viewed the program.

The riots by Beatle fans were now being covered routinely in the British newspapers.

The Beatles toured Britain from November 1 through December 13. This time there was no other headliner on the tour with them. Peter Jay & The Jaywalkers and the Brook Brothers rounded out the bill.

In November 1963 George Harrison made his debut as a songwriter with the composition *Don't Bother Me* on the group's second British album, *With The Beatles*. Previously, only John and Paul had written songs for The Beatles.

Despite their success in England, The Beatles were still virtually unknown in America. There were no Beatle records on the music charts in the U.S., although several of their first English singles had been issued on the Swan and VJ labels for American audiences.

Whatever airplay on radio stations these singles might have had, they failed to bring any fame to The Beatles.

All of this changed, however, when New York radio station WMCA broadcast The Beatles' *I Want To Hold Your Hand* on December 29, 1963 at 12:50 p.m.

It was the first Beatles' record to get important airplay in the U.S. and preceded by only a little more than a month The Beatles' arrival in New York.

If 1963 was the year in which The Beatles' conquered England, 1964 was the year in which they took America and the rest of the world by storm.

They began with a three-week performance in Paris at the Olympia Theatre in January. Then on February 7, 1964 they flew to New York on Pam Am Flight 101 from London, arriving at Kennedy International Airport.

Some 10,000 screaming New York teenagers greeted The Beatles when they landed. There was coverage on all the radio and television stations of their press conference at the airport.

The chaos at the airport was to become standard from then on wherever the group arrived.

The high point of The Beatles' visit to New York was their appearance on *The Ed Sullivan Show* on February 9 and 16, 1964. Some 50,000 people wanted seats in the television theatre, which accommodated only 728. Tickets became impossible to get at any price.

An audience of some 73 million people was estimated to have viewed The Beatles on the *Sullivan Show*. This was nearly three times larger than their audience in England the previous November for the Royal Variety Performance. America was clearly the big time for The Beatles.

From New York the group moved on to Washington, D.C., where they were greeted by some 20,000 fans.

They did their first concert in the U.S. in Washington at the Coliseum. Many of the fans pelted The Beatles with jelly beans. They had heard about a complaint George once made that John had eaten all of his "jelly babies." What the American teens didn't know was that English "jelly babies" are soft candies, unlike the much harder American jelly beans. The Beatles never enjoyed this particular aspect of Beatlemania because it hurt to get pelted with jelly beans!

The Beatles returned to New York and appeared live at Carnegie Hall for two performances on Lincoln's Birthday, February 12, 1964. The relatively small theatre seated only about 2,800 people.

It was reportedly impossible to hear anything that The

Beatles actually sang that night because there was simply too much screaming from the fans in the audience.

The Beatles are said to have received only $6500 for their performances at Carnegie Hall. Promoter Sid Bernstein made the deal by telephone from New York to London. He later went on to promote all of their New York shows but one.

To recuperate from their Carnegie Hall performances, The Beatles took a brief vacation in Miami. On February 25, 1964 George turned 21.

In March 1964 The Beatles began filming their first motion picture, *A Hard Day's Night.* It was produced by Walter Shenson for United Artists. Richard Lester directed, and the script was written by Liverpool playwright Alun Owen. The title came from an expression used by Ringo from time to time.

It was on the first day of filming of *A Hard Day's Night* that George met Pattie Boyd, who had done a television commercial for Smith's Crisps (potato chips) that Richard Lester directed.

He had, in turn, given her a brief role in The Beatles' movie. George and Pattie were married on January 21, 1966 at Epsom Register Office in Surrey, England.

On March 23, 1964 John Lennon's first book, *In His Own Write,* was published. On March 31 The Beatles dominated the music charts. *Can't Buy Me Love* was Number One. *Twist And Shout* was second. *She Loves You* was Number Three. *I Want To Hold Your Hand* came in fourth. *Please, Please Me* was Number Five. Other Beatle songs held positions 16, 44, 49, 69, 78, 84 and 88!

On May 6, 1964 a television film about The Beatles, *Around The Beatles,* was shown in Britain.

It was repeated on June 8. The Beatles were in Denmark for concerts from June 4-6. On June 8 they began a tour of Hong Kong, Australia and New Zealand.

Ringo, however, was suffering from tonsillitis and missed both the Denmark and Hong Kong performances.

A Hard Day's Night had its world premiere—a Royal Premiere—at the London Pavilion Theatre on July 6, 1964.

The film was very well received. From August 19 to September 20 The Beatles toured the U.S. and Canada. They followed that with a British tour with Mary Wells from October 9-November 10.

The following month Ringo had his tonsils removed at University College Hospital in London. It wasn't the greatest way to end the year for Ringo, but he managed to get 1965 off to a good start with his marriage to Maureen Cox on February 11 at Caxton Hall, London.

From February 22-March 12, 1965 The Beatles were filming their second motion picture, *Help!* in the Bahamas.

They moved to Austria for more filming on March 13, and then returned to England for the remaining production work on *Help!* during April and May.

On June 12, 1965 it was announced that The Beatles were to be awarded the MBE, making them each a Member of the Order of the British Empire. Many older Englishmen who already received similar honors returned them or complained about The Beatles being added to the honors list.

The Beatles, in turn, weren't very impressed with their MBEs, but they did accept them when they were presented by Her Majesty Queen Elizabeth II at Buckingham Palace on October 26.

The Beatles toured France, Italy and Spain from June 20 to July 4, 1965.

John's second book, *A Spaniard In The Works,* was published on June 24.

Their second movie, *Help!* had its world and Royal Premiere at the London Pavilion on July 29, 1965. From August 13 to September 1 The Beatles returned to

America for their third visit.

This time their tour brought them to New York, where they taped *The Ed Sullivan Show* with Cilla Black for telecast on September 9 and two performances at Shea Stadium before crowds of more than 55,000 people; Toronto; Atlanta; Houston, Chicago; Minneapolis; Portland; Los'Angeles; San Diego and San Francisco. In most of these cities they appeared at baseball stadiums, attracting enormous audiences for every performance.

As a result, although this tour was about half as long as their previous 1964 American visit had been, it was substantially more profitable than the earlier one.

On September 13, 1965, Ringo and Maureen's son Zak Starkey was born at 8 a.m. in Los Angeles.

Candlestick Park in San Francisco was the scene of their last concert on that tour on August 29. They flew back to London the next day.

In September, 1966, John Lennon began two months of filming in Germany and Spain for the picture *How I Won The War*. It marked his debut as a movie actor without the three other Beatles.

George vacationed in India in October, 1966, and took sitar lessons there from Ravi Shankar. His travels with Shankar interested him in yoga and Eastern music. This culminated in *Ravi Shankar's Musical Festival From India* at the Albert Hall in London on September 23, 1974, in which George participated.

While John was working in Germany and Spain and George was in India on a holiday, Ringo was relaxing in Spain. In November, Paul was working on the music for the movie *The Family Way,* produced by the Boulting Brothers.

After completing the score he, too, went on vacation, first in France and Spain, and then in Nairobi, Kenya.

The Beatles returned to London in December 1966 to record more music. Their single *Penny Lane/Strawberry Fields Forever* was released in England on February 17,

1967.

Two months later Paul returned to the U.S. to help Jane Asher celebrate her 21st birthday in Denver.

The Beatles' LP *Sgt. Pepper's Lonely Hearts Club Band* was released in England on June 1, 1967. In August George and Patti came to America to attend Ravi Shankar's Hollywood Bowl concert in Los Angeles.

While there, George wrote *Blue Jay Way* for The Beatles' album *Magic Mystery Tour*.

On June 25, 1967 The Beatles were presented to a worldwide television audience of some 150 million people. The program *Our World* presented a live telecast of The Beatles recording their songs *All You Need Is Love* and *Baby You're a Rich Man* at the EMI Studios in London.

The Maharishi Mahesh Yogi came to Great Britain in mid-August 1967. Patti Harrison had become a member of a group called the Spiritual Regeneration Movement in February 1967.

She had become interested in Indian religions after traveling to India with George in October 1966.

Through a girlfriend, Patti attended a lecture dealing with transcendental meditation and became interested enough to sign up for a seminar on the subject to be held that summer in Bangor, North Wales.

Newspaper ads in the London papers in August 1967 announced that the Maharishi would be speaking in London and then going on to Bangor to lecture at the conference there.

At Patti's urging George decided to attend, and personally urged John, Paul, and Ringo to do so. They all went to hear the Maharishi speak at the London Hilton Hotel on August 24, 1967. Following that they accepted his invitation to proceed with him to Bangor.

So many fans saw them off at London's Euston Station that Cynthia Lennon was unable to get through to board the train!

IX

THE GUIDING SPIRIT,
BRIAN EPSTEIN, IS DEAD

Brian Epstein was only thirty-two years old on August 27, 1967. But death claimed him that day in his apartment on London's Chapel Street.

It was a holiday weekend in Britain and Brian wanted to spend it with friends at that country home in Sussex.

When unable to round up enough people to make for a weekend of partying in Sussex, he decided to return to London late at night. He slept most of the next day, Saturday, but telephoned an old friend late in the day and made arrangements to return by train to the country.

When he never showed up his friends and staff at the London apartment were alarmed. A doctor was sent to Chapel Street and discovered that Brian had died in his bed.

The Beatles were notified of Brian's death immediately. They were with the Maharishi in Bangor at the time.

On September 8, 1967 it was officially ruled by a coroner's jury that Brian's death had been accidental. He had been taking a drug called Carbitral for a long time.

The cumulative effect of bromide in this drug was said to have killed him, particularly since he had been given to taking more of it than he should have.

On October 17, 1967 a memorial service was held for Brian Epstein at the New London Synagogue on Abbey Road in St. John's Wood, London.

The synagogue is not very far from the EMI Studios, where The Beatles had made all of their records to that time.

Unfortunately, Brian's death was a milestone in the

career of The Beatles. There has been considerable speculation over the years as to whether the group would have broken up if Brian had still been alive to guide them.

The Beatles spent the fall of 1967 working on their color television film, *Magical Mystery Tour,* for presentation on BBC-TV in December. They were involved in its scripting, casting, filming and editing.

The result was a television production that was initially telecast on December 26, 1967 in England, and throughout Europe, South America, Australia and Japan. It has since been seen in the United States as a theatrical film. It is one of the few things The Beatles ever did that was not well received by the critics.

As 1967 ended Ringo was in Rome acting in the motion picture *Candy.* On December 7, 1967 The Beatles opened their Apple Boutique at 94 Baker Street in London. Paul McCartney and Jane Asher were engaged on Christmas Day 1967. John flew to Morocco on December 29 for a short New Year's vacation.

On January 5, 1968 *Magical Mystery Tour* was shown in color on the British network BBC-2. Its earlier Christmas showing had been in black & white on BBC-1, the large British network that at the time had no color facilities but reached many more viewers than the BBC's smaller UHF network, BBC-2.

George was working on the soundtrack for the motion picture *Wonderwall.* He had begun composing its score in London in December 1967, and then spent 10 days in Bombay, India, doing additional composing and recording.

John joined George in India and the two of them stayed for the full three-month course given by the Maharishi at his Academy in Rishikesh.

They were there from February through April 1968. Ringo had attended for about two weeks before returning to England. Paul had stayed on for a short time after Ringo left, but he, too, decided to call it quits.

In February 1968 The Bealtes formed Apple Corps Ltd., an ambitious company intended to take over from the group's earlier company, Beatles, Ltd.

Among the subsidiaries of Apple Corps, Ltd. were: Apple Electronics, Apple Films, Apple Music Publishing, Apple Wholesale, Apple Retail, Apple Television and Apple Records. The first Apple project other than the boutique which opened in London on December 7, 1967, was The Beatles' film *Magical Mystery Tour.*

The cartoon movie *Yellow Submarine,* featuring animated Beatle characters and The Beatles' music, was released on July 17, 1968. In August, George wrote *Sour Milk Sea,* which was recorded by Jackie Lomax. November brought the release of The Beatles' *White Album* and George's own *Wonderwall* LP.

1968 ended with John and Yoko Ono filming *Rock 'n' Roll Circus,* which was never commercially released.

1969 got underway with The Beatles starting to work on their album *Let It Be.* On February 3, 1969 it was announced that Allen Klein had been appointed to handle The Beatles' and Apple's business affairs.

March was a month for Beatle weddings. John, who had divorced Cynthia, married Yoko Ono on March 20 at the Registrar's Office in Gibraltar.

They spent their seven-day honeymoon holding a "bed-in" at the Amsterdam Hilton Hotel. Paul, who had been engaged but never married to Jane Asher, tied the knot with Linda Eastman on March 12 at London's Marylebone Register Office.

Ringo starred in the motion picture *The Magic Christian,* which was in production between March and May 1969. It had its world premiere on December 12, 1969.

John and Yoko's movie *Rape — Part II* had its world

premiere on March 31, 1969. On April 22 John officially had his middle name changed from Winston to Ono in honor of his new wife.

George's experimental album, *Electronic Sounds,* was released in May 1969. The following month he produced Billy Preston's international hit single, *That's The Way God Planned It.* In August the LP *Hara Krishna Mantra* by Radha Krishna Temple, produced by George, was released.

September saw the release of The Beatles' *Abbey Road* album. The same month *An Evening With John & Yoko* was presented at the New Cinema Club in London. Four of the couple's movies were featured—*Two Virgins, Smile, Honeymoon* and *Self Portrait.*

In October 1969 George's *Something* was released as a single, and went on to become a major hit. In December George toured the United Kingdom with Delaney & Bonnie, trading guitar chores with Eric Clapton.

March 1970 saw the release of the second album by Radha Krishna Temple, *Govinda,* produced by George.

On April 10, 1970 a newpaper story appeared stating that The Beatles were going to break up. The story was denied by Apple, which said that it was not true that Paul McCartney was planning to leave The Bealtes.

Paul's first solo album, *McCartney,* was released in April. Ringo's initial LP as an individual artist, *Sentimental Journey,* came out the following month. A second LP by Ringo, *Beaucoups of Blue,* was issued in September.

On May 20, 1970 The Beatles' third theatrical motion picture as a group, *Let It Be,* had its world premiere at the London Pavilion. The picture, distributed by United Artists, was produced by Neil Aspinall, The Beatles' original road manager. It was directed by Michael Lindsay-Hogg.

George's first solo album, *All Things Must Pass,* was brought out in December 1970, the same month in which

John's initial solo LP, *Plastic Ono Band,* appeared.

1970 ended with Paul McCartney suing to dissolve The Beatles. The defendants in the action he brought were John Ono Lennon of Ascot, Berkshire; George Harrison of Henley-on-Thames, Berkshire; Richard Starkey (Ringo Starr) of Highgate, London, and Apple Corps. of Savile Row, London.

Throughout January and February 1971 the newspapers were filled with reports concerning how much—or, rather, how little—money The Beatles actually had.

On March 12, 1971 an official receiver, Douglas Spooner, was appointed by the High Court in London to receive and manage The Beatles' business activities until the legal suit brought by Paul was settled.

John, George and Ringo appealed against the appointment of the receiver on March 19, but withdrew their appeal on March 26. They stated through their attorney, Morris Finer, that they now wanted to explore ways in which Paul could take himself out of their Beatles partnership by agreement.

In April 1971 George wrote *Try Some Buy Some* and produced it with Phil Spector. On May 15, 1971 the Filmmaker's Fortnight Festival was held in Cannes, France, featuring films by John and Yoko.

Paul's album *RAM* was released in May 1971. He ended the year by putting out another solo album, *Wild Life,* in December.

George put together two historic charity concerts for Bangla Desh on July 31 at Madison Square Garden in New York City. Among those participating with him were Bob Dylan, Ringo Starr, Leon Russell, Billy Preston, Badfinger, Eric Clapton and Ravi Shankar.

In September five films by John and Yoko were features at the Art Spectrum in London. They included *Cold Turkey, Ballad of John & Yoko, Give Peace A Chance, Instant Karma* and *Up Your Legs.*

September 1971 also saw the release of the album *Imagine* by John.

Two of Ringo's motion pictures had their world premieres in November 1971. *200 Motels* was released on Novemeber 10. *Blindman* came out on November 15. On November 23 the movie *Raga,* featuring George, had its world premiere.

In January 1972 George's *Concert for Bangla Desh* triple album was released. Out of this stemmed the Material World Charitable Foundation, founded by George in March 1973.

The Beatles Fan Club officially shut up shop on February 8, 1972, apparently convinced that The Beatles were over and done with as a group.

The film version of the *Concert for Bangla Desh* had its world premiere on March 23, 1972. In March and April Ringo was busy with the filming of *Born To Boogie,* which he directed. It had its world premiere on December 18, 1972.

John appeared on *One To One,* a benefit concert for mentally retarded children, on August 31, 1972.

In August and September Paul toured Northern England and Southern Scotland with his new band Wings. He became the first Beatle to tour since 1966.

In the fall of 1972 George Harrison began filming *Little Malcolm And His Struggle Against The Eunuchs,* for which he was Executive Producer. Between October 1972 and January 1973 Ringo was busy starring in the film *That'll Be The Day,* which had its world premiere on April 12, 1973.

John and Yoko's movie *Imagine* had its world premiere on December 23, 1972.

On March 30, 1973 John, George and Ringo terminated their managerial contract with Allen Klein and his company ABKCO.

In April 1973 Paul's album *Red Rose Speedway* was released. He followed that with the LP *Band On The Run* in November.

George's *Give Me Love* single was released on May 14, 1973. His album *Living In The Material World* was released shortly thereafter on May 29.

On June 29 the James Bond movie *Live And Let Die,* with title music by Paul, had its world premiere.

John, George and Ringo recorded together for the first time in four years on July 10, 1973 when they cut John's *I'm The Greatest* for Ringo's LP *Ringo,* which was released on October 15, 1973.

October aslo saw the release of John's LP *Mind Games.* In November John, George and Ringo sued Allen Klein, who in turn sued them.

George returned to India in February 1974. In May George formed Dark Horse Records. The same month saw the world premiere of *Son Of Dracula,* produced by and starring Ringo.

The following month brought the world premiere of *Little Malcolm And His Struggle Against The Eunuchs,* for which George was Executive Producer. It captured the Silver Bear Gold Medal at the Atlanta Film Festival in August.

On September 6, 1974 George announced plans for an extensive concert tour of Europe, which he did in September and October. On September 23 he participated in the Ravi Shankar Festival at London's Albert Hall. He then went on to do concerts in Paris, Brussels, Frankfurt, Munich and Copenhagen.

September was also the month in which John's album *Walls And Bridges* was released. November 1974 brought the release of Ringo's LP *Goodnight Vienna.*

George returned to North America in November for a tour. His album *Dark Horse* was released on December 2, 1974.

On January 9, 1975 the last legal links between The Beatles were dissolved in court. John's album *Rock 'n' Roll* was released on February 17, 1975. A single by John,

Stand By Me, was released on March 10, 1975.

Paul McCartney and Wings' album, *Venus And Mars,* was released on May 27, 1975. A single, *Listen To What The Man Said,* had been released shortly before on May 19. Another single, *Letting Go,* was released on September 22. It was followed by the single *Venus And Mars Rock Show* on November 3.

Ringo and his wife Maureen were divorced in July 1975 after ten years of marriage.

George's album *Extra Texture (Read All About It)* was issued in September 1975. The next month John and Yoko's first child, Sean Ono Lennon, arrived.

John's LP *Shaved Fish* was released on October 22, 1975. Ringo's album *Blast From Your Past* was issued on November 20, 1975.

Ringo's film *Lisztomania* had its world premiere on October 10, 1975. In November Paul began a major world tour with Wings of England, Australia and Europe.

In February 1976 promoter Bill Sargent stunned the world by offering The Beatles *$50 million* if they would do a single performance together. They never accepted his offer.

Paul's LP *Wings At The Speed Of Sound* came out in March 1976. From May 3 — June 23, 1976 Wings toured North America. Paul appeared on a concert stage in the U.S. for the first time since The Beatles' final American show in San Francisco's Candlestick Park on August 29, 1966.

June 11, 1976 marked the first re-release of Beatles' songs by Capitol Records (other than the 1962-66 and 1967-70 anthologies issued in April 1973). The album, *Rock 'n' Roll Music,* was backed by what Capitol said was the largest and most extensive marketing campaign in its history, and possibly the biggest ever seen in the music business.

On July 27, 1976 the population of the United States

was officially increased by one 35-year-old former Beatle. The American government had given up its efforts to deport John Lennon, and granted him a green "permanent resident alien" card. Clutching his wife, Yoko Ono, John remarked, "As usual there is a great woman behind every idiot."

October 1976 saw the release of George's album *The Best of George Harrison*. In December Paul's *Wings Over America* came out.

Ringo's first album for release on the Atlantic Records label, Ringo's *Rotogravure,* came out in September 1976. In November George's *Thirty-Three & 1/3* his first LP on the Dark Horse label, was released.

A stage play called *Beatlemania* came to Broadway's Winter Garden Theatre in April 1977. It became an instant smash hit thanks to its four musicians who were made up and dressed to (somewhat)resemble The Beatles while singing and playing Beatle songs.

The show was produced by David Krebs and Steve Leber, and had disc jockey Murray The K—Murray Kaufman, The Fifth Beatle—as a special consultant. The four stars of the show were Justin McNeil (as Ringo), Mitch Weissman (as Paul), Leslie Franklin (as George) and Joe Pecorino (as John).

On May 4, 1977 Capital Records released *The Beatles At The Hollywood Bowl,* the first official live Beatles album ever. It was the first never-before-released Beatles recording to appear in the U.S. in the seven years since the group split up.

Paul and Linda McCartney welcomed their first son, James Louis, in September 1977.

Ringo's LP, *Ringo, The 4th*, on the Atlantic Records label, was released in November.

Filming began in the fall of 1977 on Universal Studios' *Beatles 4 Ever,* concerning a group of New Jersey teenagers who travel to New York City to see The Beatles' debut on *The Ed Sullivan Show* on February 9, 1964.

The picture, whose title was later changed to *I Want To Hold Your Hand,* revolved around how the teens' lives are affected and changed by The Beatles. Carrie Fisher of *Star Wars* fame was originally announced as the film's star, but she dropped out of the project due to "scheduling difficulties."

She was replaced by Susan New man. Others in the cast included Nancy Allen, Bobby Di Cicco, Marc McClure, Theresa Saldana and Wendie Jo Sperber.

Capitol Records brought out another album of re-issued Beatles' material, *Love Songs,* on October 24, 1977. It featured 25 of the group's classic songs about love in a beautifully-packaged double album complete with a booket containing the lyrics to each record. The album had a leather-like look and texture to its jacket, which featured a gold-embossed photograph of The Beatles by Richard Avedon. Another Avedon photo was printed on the two inside pages of the album jacket.

Much of the material on the *Love Songs* album was culled from albums that were from The Beatles' early period. Many of the songs, themselves, had been buried in these LPs that aren't found in the record collections of latter-day Beatle devotees.

Filming wound up in December 1977 on another Beatles-oriented motion picture, *Sgt. Pepper's Lonely Hearts Club Band,* starring Peter Frampton and The Bee Gees. The film's producer, Robert Stigwood, had been hired by Brian Epstein in 1967 to serve as co-managing director of Nems Enterprises, the company Brian had established in 1961 to manage The Beatles.

The film, which features all singing without any dialogue, was produced for release by Universal Studios.

1977 ended with the show *Beatlemania* being booked in Los Angeles' Shubert Theatre for a run of at least 19 weeks. The original New York cast made the move to L.A. with the new production.

Others took over in New York to keep the Broadway production going. Plans were for a national road company and an international company to tour the Far East and other parts of the world.

A whole new generation of Beatles fans—many of whom were very young children in the mid-'60s and had no personal memories of The Beatles—was now being given a chance to see what The Beatles had looked like and to hear what they had sounded like. Of course, everyone knew that those four men on stage were just actors. They were not The Beatles, themselves. But did that make any difference? Apparently not. To those who came to see the show the effect was similar to having The Beatles up there on the stage. In fact, to many there was only one important difference—this time you could actually hear what they were singing!

X

THE BEATLES K.O.
ELVIS PRESLEY

The advent of rock'n'roll in the 1950s was a revolution unlike any musical introduction the world has known. It's effect on society was immediate. And very lasting. Its impact on radio, television, movies, and the stage has survived nearly three decades. It appears that it will continue to be the dominant musical force of the 1980s and beyond.

Rock'n'roll's influence has been greatest on radio. The dawn of rock's great popularity on the airwaves began with Elvis Presley. When he burst on the scene in 1956, an era unlike any other began for the medium.

On many hundreds of major stations throughout the United States and Canada, broadcasting underwent a dramatic metamorphosis. Soap operas, dramas, and lengthy newscasts went into decline. Eventually, many stations did completely away with the soaps and dramas. Rock became standard fare on AM radio and, with the arrival and broad expansion of FM its takeover of the ozone was complete.

Eight years after the Elvis Presley craze, yet another upheaval swept radio, as well as TV, movies, and the stage. The Beatles' impact on the entertainment world was every bit as awesome as was Presley's. Just as Presley had helped the great era of Top 40 radio reach unprecedented heights, so did the Beatles rouse a new wave of interest in the broadcast medium.

To gauge the impact and influence the Beatles exerted on radio, bestselling author Martin A. Grove, an expert on the group from Liverpool, interviewed one of America's leading radio programmers, Rick Sklar.

When the Beatles landed in New York City in 1964,

that metropolis' radio stations had first crack at them. Among the first to air the Beatles was WABC, whose programming was conducted by Sklar. Today, Sklar is Vice President of Programming for ABC Radio throughout the country.

Sklar is one of the most knowledgeable sources about Beatlemania and was sought out by Marty Grove as an expert to comment on the influence the Beatles have exerted on the music scene, as well as the world at large. The occasion for that interview was in preparation for Grove's book, *Beatle Madness* (published in 1978 by Manor Books).

The launching platform for that tome was rooted in the sudden revival of interest in the Fab Four and the hot pronouncements in *Rolling Stone* magazine that John, Paul, George, and Ringo were to make an appearance in the movie, *Sgt. Pepper's Lonely Hearts Club Band*.

Grove got the interview going with Sklar by asking him to comment about the "tremendous revival of interest" in the Beatles.

Sklar responded that he didn't believe interest in the Beatles ever went away entirely. He went on to say: "If you look at the playlists of radio stations, very very few groups from the early and mid-60s remain in the record libraries of what you would call contemporary or rock music radio stations. Most of them tend to concentrate on the last half-dozen years or so, which would preclude most of The Beatles' music. And yet, that rule doesn't hold for The Beatles. Beatle material has stayed alive and active all through this time."

The interview then proceeded in this sequence:

GROVE: Is there a nostalgia factor involved here, too?

SKLAR: I think after a decade or so has past in any field you begin to get a nostalgia revival of what went on a decade ago. If you go back ten years, well you're into the height of The Beatles' popularity. So it's just about due at this time. People like to have their memories tickled about ten years back. That's about where we are right now. It's perfectly logical that this would happen in the case of The Beatles since they never really faded away altogether in their music. It's all the more intense an experience and will be, I suppose, as the music continues, the motion pictures begin to come out in quantity and the live presentations of their material—such as the *Beatlemania* show and similar revival ideas—come about.

GROVE: *When The Beatles first appeared on the scene in 1964 did you have any idea that they would become almost an institution?*

SKLAR: No, and neither did they. I say that because I've talked to them about the first appearance they did in the United States. They deliberately selected a small concert hall—relatively small compared to what was available for rock groups—because they wanted to be sure of a sell-out. They had no idea that it was going to get that big in this country. They thought it might, but they didn't know for sure. They weren't going to take any chances so they used Carnegie Hall in New York City, which seats under 2,800.

GROVE: *What was their first performance at Carnegie Hall like?*

SKLAR: I can tell you that from the very beginning their reception at Carnegie Hall characterized the respose of audiences ever since. There was total hysteria and a frantic reaction by the crowd. At that very first concert you never heard a note of what they were singing! The audience's screams were just too loud. No one ever heard a single note of that concert.

GROVE: *How did the frenzy for The Beatles compare to the frenzy that there had been for Elvis Presley in the '50s?*

SKLAR: Well, the Beatles' frenzy was much more in the nature of absolute hysteria. When Presley performed, oh, there was shouting and screaming and cheering. But you could hear Presley. They were still an audience, and they settled back in their seats. But for The Beatles there was just total hysteria. There's been nothing even comparable to it. The only thing comparable to it in any way at all was the reaction in the earlier decades to Frank Sinatra. But the early Sinatra with the swooning of bobbysoxers at the Paramount Theatre in New York was mild compared to this. This was a total exercise in mass hysteria—fainting, screaming and flashbulbs going off. An intensity that had probably not been seen in American show business ever before.

GROVE: Why do you think audiences need to have an outlet like The Beatles, like Elvis, like Sinatra, or like Valentino if you go way back? Why this need for being able to become hysterical in public and profess your love for a certain personality or group?

SKLAR: In our everyday lives civilized society has put almost an emotional straightjacket on some of the inner drives that are part of our biological inheritance. We tend to keep these things in great check. It is only when that same society legitimizes in some way the act of bursting out of these constraints that most people would be able to go along with it. It's easier for young people than for adults. So given this legitimizing by society of an act of total hysteria—you know, it was now the consensus that you can act this way at a Beatles concert—the restraints have been cut loose and out comes the reaction.

GROVE: The Beatles started out doing a kind of music that was very different from what they wound up doing. How would you characterize The Beatles' music by periods? How did it change?

SKLAR: I think their early stuff was a lot less sophisticated, although musically it was excellent. Many people take the *Revolver* album as the point in time when they started to get really serious with their music and decided to see how many areas they could branch out into. I think there was an early simplified approach. The *I Want To Hold Your Hand* and *Please, Please Me* stuff. Then we began to get into their real attempts to become lyrically and musically more serious artists. They decided to see how far they could go with popular music, exploring underlying psychological manifestations or social commentaries on the scene, experimenting with more complex musical forms. By the time you reach *Sgt. Pepper* and the *Magical Mystery Tour,* you're dealing with social commentary on the human condition, on people's lives and what's behind their actions and reactions, philosophy of life, which John Lennon in particular was into in a serious philosophical way and George Harrison in a more naive, evangelistic or simplistic way. What is life all about? What are we really doing here? What are we?—This sort of thing began coming into their songs.

GROVE: What about Paul McCartney? Did he have any similar serious interests?

SKLAR: Yes, he's serious. But McCartney always retained a very strong commercial sense of what approaches will sell best. Later on when we see him working on something of his own like *Silly Love Songs,* that was McCartney. He wanted to write silly love songs, really! He has a very commercial sense about him. When they worked as a team, the Lennon/McCartney team, all this was synthesized into a very powerful group. As a solo artist Paul seems to have had the most commercial success.

I think he's the one with the most innate understanding of what it is that really sells the music, what they really go for in both melody and lyrics and in the arrangements. He's got a sense of the public pulse, and I think it explains why when the group worked together almost every song clicked so well. Each one contributed something to it. When you take them apart, if you have nothing else you've got to have a portion of talent and a sense of commercialism. If you've got both of those you can keep going on your own. I think he's got that sense of what sells commercially.

GROVE: Do you think that that was one of the reasons for the split between The Beatles?

SKLAR: Oh, no. I'm certainly in no way qualified to hypothesize on why the split occurred and why any reconciliation would be so difficult. Obviously, there would be tremendous financial considerations. Although, as the years go by I imagine those get less and less. It would be easier to do it today as all the past arrangements become untangled over the years. Though whether emotionally they could get together again I don't know.

GROVE: There was a lot of speculation recently about a group Capitol Records has called Klaatu, and whether it is really The Beatles recording together in secret under another name. Do you think that's the case?

SKLAR: No. That's just some promotion man's dream.

GROVE: It's amazing how much has been written on the subject.

SKLAR: Yeah.

GROVE: What do you think The Batles' real effect on other groups and on music in the '60s and the '70s has been?

SKLAR: There were many effects. Initially they set a new plateau for musical excellence. They were the advance wave of a whole invasion of dozens and dozens of British groups.

GROVE: Why did The Beatles succeed and all those other British groups—like Gerry & The Pacemakers, The Dave Clark Five, even The Rolling Stones—fail to score as significantly. The same kind of lightning that struck for The Beatles never struck for anybody else in the British invasion. Why?

SKLAR: To succeed on a permanent basis to the point where your material becomes part of that permanent solid gold library, you really have to have substance and not just a facade. Whenever there are originators and imitators there is substance and there is facade. Frequently, the imitators are only the facade. Four people come over from England and they do a great job here. Now more groups come over from England, but the quality isn't the same. The polish isn't there. The depth isn't there. Sure, for a while you get swept up in the general hysteria of any group from Britain. People want to see them and hear them. But, unless you're doing something very unique and very good like The Rolling Stones, and you are your own group, you're not going to last. You're not going to go down in history. You don't get many of them that really stuck with it in the heads of the public.

GROVE: One of the influences on The Beatles was probably Elvis Presley. The way things ultimately worked out, the arrival of The Beatles knocked Presley off the music charts for a long time.

SKLAR: That's exactly what happened. In 1964 The Beatles arrived. In 1964 Presley left the Top 100 charts. It's all there in musical history if you go back and look at the charts.

GROVE: Why do you think that was? Why didn't the public have room enough for both Presley and The Beatles?

SKLAR: Well, I don't know that the public consciously thought of it that way. But there is usually a central top group or artist in any given time, and then there are others. I guess there can only be one King at a time—a person or a group. But in many ways, while Presley didn't have the hits anymore, he retained a lot of following in many parts of the country. People simply put him in one category and The Beatles in another. But there's no question that, overall, The Beatles came to dominate the charts. In that first year they had 29 singles on the market. Now some of these were different versions of the same song. But there were 29 singles in 1964 one way or another in the American market by The Beatles. Now that's incredible. It's unheard of. It's never been surpassed by anyone.

GROVE: So they really were a productive team.

SKLAR: Oh, sure. They just overwhelmed in sheer numbers as well as quality. Quality and quantity. When you get them both it's hard to beat.

GROVE: What did you think of The Beatles when they branched out of the recording industry and started going into motion pictures?

SKLAR: They didn't stick by any rules. They were very innovative in their films and in their visual work. They let a lot of humor get into it. You've got to be pretty confident when you branch out into humor. They worked their songs into their movies, and wrote new material for each film that came along. I thought that their films were excellent.

GROVE: I've recently been going through stacks of photographs of The Beatles, taken over a period of probably 10 years. Some of them are included in this book. As you look at their pictures it is, in many cases, actually difficult to identify the people in the latter period photographs with the people in the earlier photos. They physically do not look close to being the same. If you look at such a wide range of pictures you will find that there's even a middle period in which the same people don't resemble the people in the late period or the early period! Why do you think all four of them went through so many physical changes?

SKLAR: There's no question that they did go through these changes. There's no question the changes were real in terms of the productivity of the work they were doing, the type of work, their physical appearances, their outlook on life and that changes like these do not normally occur in an individual or a group. In fact, most artists try to retain over the years a certain youthfulness that they had earlier. They literally try to present the same face to the public. I would imagine that—and I can only speculate here—the changes were caused by the intensity of the public reaction to them and its effect upon them. This was a very very unusual experience for a human being to go through, and here four of them went through it. The thought of public adulation, of public reaction—reserved in Ancient Rome for the Emperor, in Ancient Egypt for the Pharoah! It's very rare that you get this kind of a reaction by a public to a human being, placing them in a semi-Godlike status. That has to have some kind of effect after a time on the individuals involved, who after all are mere mortals. You know, they're people like us. And yet they're subject to this almost deification in the generation in which they're playing. In that ten-year period this has to have an effect. Perhaps this is what we're seeing when we see them go through these intense changes unlike other groups of artists.

GROVE: What are they like today?

SKLAR: I'd say that Paul has retained more of the artist-to-public posture of the four of them. More of that artist-to-pubic posture that was there in the days when they were performing as a group. The others, I think, are more introspective and more private in many ways in their thoughts. Certainly, I've shared some of John's thinking, and have had some talks with George, and have met Paul a few times when he's been in New York. I think they are more private individuals now than they were. I know John looks back at The Beatles as another entity. He looks upon the group not as a former member, but as if they were something else. He looks from the outside looking in at those four people who existed as The Beatles.

GROVE: Are they comfortable today as artists? They made this major move away from being a group. Was it the right move for them?

SKLAR: I think Paul is most comfortable in continuing work as an artist. I think John is very much a family man right now. I really can't tell you precisely how he's thinking and feeling at this moment.

GROVE: With the untimely death of Elvis Presley there was an enormous groundswell of interest in his life—books, magazines, television programs, film revivals, newspaper coverage from coast-to-coast, a tremendous outpouring of love from his fans. What do you think would be the effect of one or more of The Beatles passing on? How do you think their public would react?

SKLAR: I don't even want to think about it. I just hope that they all live long, happy, healthy lives.

GROVE: Yes, of course. We all do. But we also know that for all of us the day will come.

SKLAR: Well, I would say that certainly there was this same very emotional tie between the public and a few really special artists. Certainly there is a very strong tie that exists with The Beatles. I don't know if it's as intense with all of them. And there's a difference between a single artist and members of a group. But I think it would be a sad day, you know.

GROVE: Of the four of them, who would you say is the most interesting? If you were going to have one of them as a close friend, who should it be?

SKLAR: I guess it probably would be a toss-up between John and Paul. Of course, I've spent a little more time with John than with Paul. They both seem very fascinating as creative people go.

GROVE: When The Beatles originally formed I guess it was more or less accidental that those four individuals wound up as a team. If you set out to construct the ideal rock & roll group would you have cast those four guys together to make one unit?

SKLAR: Do you mean at that time, prior to their existence as The Beatles?

GROVE: Yes. Originally. Before their fame.

SKLAR: I think it would have been a bit unlikely to come up with that combination. I don't think there was any indication that that was the type of combination that would make it.

GROVE: Going back to the early days of The Beatles, when did you as a radio programmer, first become aware that there was a group called The Beatles?

SKLAR: I believe it was 1963. Word was coming out

within the trade that there was this group in England that had caught on. There was this unusual degree of excitement that seemed to be at a greater threshold than normal. But it was tempered by the skepticism that greets every announcement that originates in promotion offices of record companies! So much of the time it's just that— promotional hoopla and nothing more. So, I guess, in an industry where they cry wolf so often when it's the real thing you really are not sure of it. But there was more than the normal amount of excitement in terms of this group.

GROVE: What kind of response did you get from the WABC audience when you first started playing I Want To Hold Your Hand, their first Capitol Records release in the U.S.?

SKLAR: Well, we check the sales of records that are exposed on the air. It sold extremely well, and there was very rapid movement upward on the music charts. I'd say it was not typical. It was unusually fast. It caught on and moved up in popularity toward the Number One slot, which it hit.

GROVE: And as it caught on was additional material from The Beatles put into release?

SKLAR: Yes. *She Loves You* came out very quickly after that. And *Please, Please Me* followed. There were more than two dozen individual Beatles' songs floating around by the end of the year.

GROVE: Would that have constituted overexposure for any other artist?

SKLAR: Absolutely.

GROVE: Why, then, do you think The Beatles were able to thrive on it?

SKLAR: For one thing, the material, generally speaking, was of better quality than you normally get. It struck a responsive nerve. It said things that people frequently think, and it said them in ways to which people could relate. Their presentation just hit the tone of the times. It filled a need.

GROVE: Are you saying, in effect, that had The Beatles come about at some other time, perhaps that wouldn't have been as fertile a period for them to work in?

SKLAR: That's right. When you get to stuff like that it's meeting the need at the proper time, and in the language of the time or in the language that's needed then. The Beatles were the group that came in, breaking with tradition by wearing their hair longer than the average person. Now until that moment in time male hair was short. This was a total break and symbolized and summed up the normal youthful rebellion that occurred when youngsters reached that teenage time when they begin to break away from some of the parental values. This seemed to be the perfect way to break away without totally rupturing things. It just suited to a tee the situation that youngsters found themselves in at that point in time. In came the long side-burns and the long hair. That was sudden, and it was The Beatles who brought it in. Yet if you look at them in those days, in their first appearances, really by the standards of the Woodstock Generation that hair wasn't really long at all. Their hair was shockingly long at the time, though. You remember they began selling Beatle wigs. And this was the first sign of long hair that eventually became the hair generation and was utilized in the musical *Hair*. Certainly, The Beatles wore their hair long. That was it. That was the other symbol— the music and the long hair. People forget that now. That was it at the time.

GROVE: So many of the other groups that formed The British Invasion of 1964 and 1965 seem to have been carbon copies of The Beatles—the same long hair, similar kind of music. None of them seem to have really succeeded in getting anywhere equally significant. Those who did have some popularity had it for only a short time, and then disappeared or regrouped. What is it that goes into the making of a truly superstar pop group?

SKLAR: The vocal talents, the material itself, the arrangements and the presentation. Of course, the more elusive characteristic is a certain charisma or electricity that is very rare and comes when all of these other elements complement one another and build a total picture without any one portion being out of sync or out of proportion. Here were four very personable young lads with a tremendous amount of talent, and really kind of shy and retiring themselves. They seemed almost fragile. I remember looking at them at their first appearance in public. I particularly remember that impression of them at Shea Statium in New York. They looked very slender and small and lost in this huge arena. One of the more interesting periods in The Beatles' career was in the late '60s, after *Abbey Road*. There were rumors then that Paul McCartney was actually dead, and that he had been secretly replaced by a lookalike singer who was carrying on in his place. I recall that there were radio programs and magazines at that time that told you clue for clue how it had all happened, how The Beatles had subtly made note of it in the illustrations on their album covers and in some of their lyrics. Even in some of their music when you listened to it played backwards! I assume that Paul wasn't dead, really. But what do you think accounts for the fact that so many people wanted to talk about that and, perhaps, believe it?

SKLAR: You know, once an idea gets started, and if it's an idea that is repeated often enough and involves something that substantial, a great many people who are naive in these areas tend to want to think there may be some substance to it. I mean, "If there wasn't, why would so many people be talking about it?" It's a self-perpetuating thing that feeds on itself and yet, of course, it's totally amiss.

GROVE: Is there any deep seated need among audiences to see their idols pass on and then to

115

memorialize them?

SKLAR: I suppose so.

GROVE: Was some of this outpouring of love and admiration for Elvis in the same vein?

SKLAR: It may be.

GROVE: There's so much hype and promotional activity in the music business involving radio stations and getting the stations to play an artist's music. The Beatles came over as a super group almost immediately. Did they get involved in any kind of station promotions?

SKLAR: It really wasn't necessary for them to be hypoed once they started. In fact, the radio stations fought one another to get exclusives on Beatle material and just get it on the air. You couldn't get enough of it. It was a rare situation.

GROVE: While this was going on The Beatles were recording new material and beginning to plot the course that they would take. Where do you see the change beginning to come about in The Beatles?

SKLAR: The *Revolver* album began to show them looking at other themes and going into more serious approaches to the music. I'd say it was about the time that *Revolver* came out (August 8, 1966 in the U.S.)

GROVE: Do you think that their music led them into different directions or were they led into different directions which they in turn reflected in their music?

SKLAR: I think as they achieved a position of such importance and leadership in the music field they took a somewhat daring step individually and collectively, because different Beatles wrote different material, of trying to deal with more serious themes. They began to look at their material as works of literature and as more serious music. To their credit, they were able to popularize this. It doesn't happe too often.

GROVE: Do you think it was international on their part? Were they conveying a philosophy that they wanted to convey?

116

SKLAR: Very definitely. They began to get into political themes eventually, religious themes and more deeply philosophical reflections on the state of man and society and the role of individuals—particularly, everyday people—who were caught up in positions of continual tedium and boredom. They also dealt with very cynical people and hypocrites. I think they really wanted to comment on the human condition. They began to do it very well in some of their music.

GROVE: Is it at all dangerous, do you think, for an individual or a group of recording artists to have such power because of their exposure to the public and the size of their audience?

SKLAR: No, I think it's a good thing that the artists involved are very sincere, genuine and well motivated. There's nothing wrong with using your musical talents to popularize more intense questions and deeper questions and raise the level of subject matter and the importance of that subject matter for what essentially is an entertainment purpose.

GROVE: What I was thinking of, in particular, was their song Revolution, where basically they came out against political revolutions. Supposing that instead of coming out in opposition to the Maoists, they had written songs in which they actually espoused the cause of social revolution and recommended it to people. Do you think that the effect of that would have been to spur their fans on to political radicalism?

SKLAR: Well, it's hard to speculate about something that hasn't been. But I think that what probably would have happened had they taken an approach that really didn't reflect the common sense of the masses in the long run is that they would have been rejected. If you go against the public grain you risk a diminishing of your importance and your popularity. One reason they were so successful is that they did strike a responsive chord. They did hit the nail on the head, so to speak, and sum up what a lot of people were thinking. If in your music you begin to come to conclusions that really do not reflect the sense of the general public, then you risk eventual obscurity. Had they taken another tack they probably would have been less popular. So I don't think it would have worked the other way and triggered people to some action.

GROVE: Then is it fair to say that the masses make the artist?

SKLAR: When an artist reflects the feelings of the masses, then the artist grows and the masses allow that artist to grow. I think that would be a realistic way of putting it.

GROVE: The group that comes to mind, of course, as being the other side of the coin from The Beatles is The Rolling Stones. Their records would seem to be a lot, more negative and a lot more potentially dangerous from a social point of view. Yet they, too, have enjoyed substantial popularity.

SKLAR: But nowhere near as great as The Beatles.

GROVE: In The Beatles' middle period—the late '60s, the period of Sgt. Pepper—there was a great deal of controversy about the content of their lyrics. For instance, about whether Lucy In The Sky With Diamonds was a song applauding drugs, and whether several other cuts on the same album were drug related. Do you think they were? Did you find those lyrics at all dangerous or borderline?

SKLAR: I really have no idea whether they were meant to be or not. What happens when you have ambiguous lyrics is that people see in them or hear in them what they want to hear. I suppose at that point in time they did have some groups in the audience that read those sort of meanings into it. But that doesn't mean that such meanings were there. Certainly there were other songs by the groups of artists that circulated at that time period that were very definite references to drugs. I'm well aware of them because of certain responsibilities to impressionable youth that broadcasters have by virtue of their decision making positions in the exposure of this material. For that reason, I'm very aware that there was some material that dealt directly with hard narcotics and drugs that was not broadcast on radio stations for that reason. But The Beatles never fell into that category.

GROVE: What would you say were the major influences on The Beatles' music as it developed over the years? One thought that comes to my mind would be the influence of the Eastern religions, for example.

SKLAR: That came late and was mixed into some of their later music in the structure of the music, the arrangements. Certainly that would be a factor. I think they read human nature very well. They were good students of psychology. They were very much influenced by human nature, and they were ready to reflect it, which is true of any really good artist. Shakespeare was a great one for reflecting on human nature and the human condition. The Beatles in their lyrics were very good at this. In some cases it was very simple. Once they had captured the audience with the simpler stuff in the earlier years they were able to lead them on because they had their confidence. They couldn't have come in at the beginning with these more sophisticated concepts.

GROVE: The Beatles achieved enormous fame. They made tremendous amounts of money. How do you think they coped with that? Do you think they coped well with being famous and super-rich?

SKLAR: Well, there appear to have been some problems. I assume the ideal way of coping with that kind of situation is to preserve as much of your earnings as possible, on the one hand, and on the other not to lose the sense of the basic day-to-day values that there are in life, which can somehow become obscured and with many artists have become obscured by sudden financial wealth. You know, the rock world is filled with artists who have flared up and made their millions and when it was all over there was no money left and very little happiness. I guess happiness would come first, and preservation of the wealth next. If they could do both and you measure them individually that way—are they happy today, and have they been able to hang on to at least some of the money— John has said, you know we're really not as rich as people think we are. That may be true. It's very tough to hang on to your money today. A lot of it goes to taxes, to agents and to the recording companies. Many, many artists start out and flare up for a few years and end up with very little of the money their talent created. I think that certainly The Beatles have managed to hold on to some of it. Some of them are still creating. Certainly Paul is, and to a lesser extent Ringo and George have at least made some attempts. John seems very happily married right now, and so does Paul. I really couldn't comment on how happy George and Ringo are at the moment.

GROVE: There is a theory in show business that no matter how successful an act is—whether it's a hit television show, a popular nightclub performer or a major recording star—that nothing can go on forever, and that sometimes the smartest thing to do is to call it quits when you're at the top of your career. In effect, this is what The Beatles did. Do you think that if they had not split up in 1970 but had resolved their differences and continued to work together, perhaps on a reduced schedule, that by now, seven years later, and fully a dozen years since the peak of their popularity, they would still be as popular and as major a factor in the entertainment world?

SKLAR: I think all we can do with a hypothesis such as that is look at other groups and look at the stature of the groups involved that stayed with it. I think that if you do have that amount of talent going for you, yes, you will continue to be successful in spite of your own doubts and fears, which even The Beatles have in this area. I think that, yes, they would have certainly remained a vital force

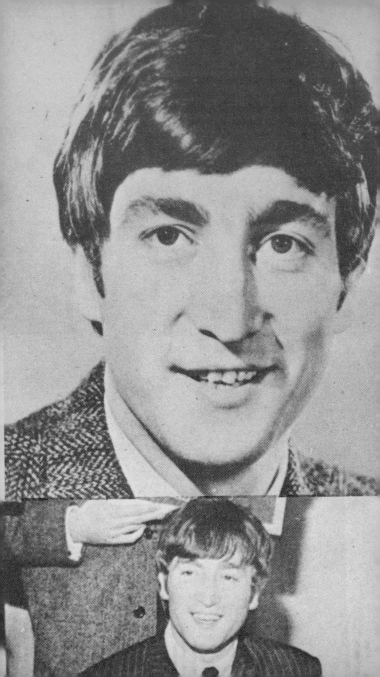

PLASTIC ONO BAND
Released: December 1970
Album SW-3372 • 8-Track 0XW-3372
Cassette 4XW-3372

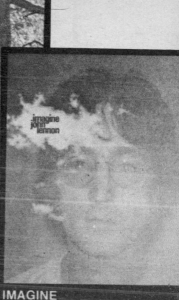

IMAGINE
Released: September 1971
Album SW-3379 • 8-Track 8XW-337
Cassette 4XW-3379 • Quad Q8W-33

JOHN LENNON
WALLS AND BRIDGES

ALLS AND BRIDGES
leased: September 1974
um SW-3416 • 8-Track 8XW-3416
ssette 4XW-3416 • Quad Q8W-3416

JOHN LENNON

MIND GAMES
Released: October 1973
Album SW-3414 • 8-Track 8XW-3

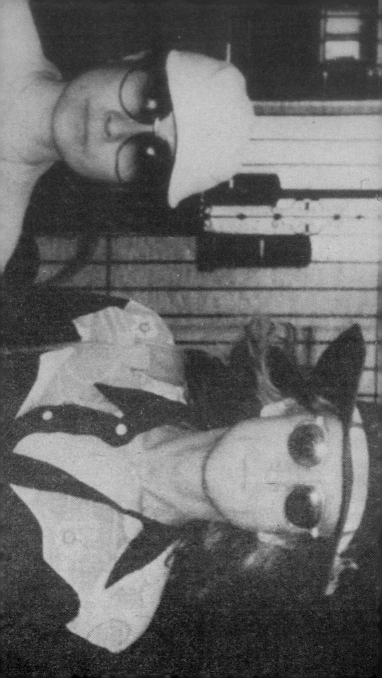

and a leading force and a very commercially successful force, one of the top groups in the business. Whether they would have stayed at the top is hard to say because you look at groups that are with us today that were with us a long, long time ago—such as The Bee Gees or The Beach Boys—ore individual artists like Presley till the end, even though he was in and out, on and off the charts and television appearances, although they are very well orchestrated and timed to avoid over-exposure. Certainly there would have been a way for The Beatles to do it. One still has this hope that there may be a way to bring them back together again at least once more.

GROVE: That is probably the thing that you hear the most. When people talk about The Beatles the discussion always will turn to "what do you think it would take to get them back together again?" Have they resolved their differences personally? Is the whole corporate mess resolved with the passage of time? Do they see each other again socially? Do they all talk to each other? Would they perform again for charity? Do you think that there is anything that anyone could do to bring them together again? These are just some of the questions people would like to have answered.

SKLAR: I think that there is the possibility that it could happen. It could be done.

GROVE: What would it take, so to speak, to put Humpty Dumpty back together again?

SKLAR: Well, if we knew the answer to that, someone could just go out and do it. I don't know that there's any magic formula or any simple answer to that.

GROVE: What do you think the chief stumbling block is?

SKLAR: There probably are personal and financial and possibly even legal stumbling blocks.

GROVE: Let's assume that the ultimate happened and The Beatles did decide to reunite. What do you think would be the result of that? What kind of music do you think would result from a reunited Beatles after a period of separation of some seven years or more?

SKLAR: It's hard to speculate on what kind of material would be produced. It certainly would sound excellent. They all still sing as well and play as well individually as they used to. I would suspect that the public would warm to them and would really be receptive to their material. I know there's the thought that there would be the inevitable comparisons between what they sound like and did now as compared with what they did before. But I think that what they actually did lyrically and musically would probably be excellent also.

GROVE: In repackaging their material as Capitol Records has been doing with the three Lps out already— and, of course, they've found a great market for all three of them—as if it were fresh and current, and to today's audiences it is, do you think Capitol has succeeded in keeping the market for The Beatles alive?

SKLAR: I don't think it's necessary for any company to keep a market alive. The market keeps itself alive and would be there whether or not they released this material.

GROVE: Then you don't think that there is greater radio airplay of Beatles songs because they come from newly released albums? Do you think that program directors of radio stations may be taking another look at The Beatles, not so much in terms of oldies but as current material because it is freshly packaged and newly re-released?

SKLAR: I don't think they'll look at it that much as new material. That might be Capitol Record's hope. But I just don't think it works that way.

GROVE: In getting to be The Beatles and in perfecting their art they started out touring. They appeared in Liverpool clubs and worked in Hamburg. Yet the first thing that went out the window when they became successful was touring. Do you think that the relationship between an artist and a live audience is an important one?

SKLAR: It's important as long as you can endure the physical problems that they had to go through. Those public appearances were very, very demanding.

GROVE: Do you think a recording artist takes something from an audience as well as gives something to it?

SKLAR: Sure. There's a rapport back and forth. But with The Beatles there was such hysteria when they appeared. It wasn't the normal back-and-forth relationship. The audience was not relating to individual selections. When The Beatles performed in public you couldn't hear them sing. They kind of had to create their material in private.

GROVE: In the early days of Beatlemania audiences seemed to have been ready for something like The Beatles to come along. They did, and they were received with open arms. The hysteria of Beatlemania followed. Do you think The Beatles, themselves, were truly aware of what was happening? Do you think they wanted this to happen the way it did? And would they have been better off if, somehow, they had tried to restrain it from mushrooming as it did?

SKLAR: Certainly they were aware of what was happening. I think that if they had tried to restrain it it wouldn't ever have been so big. The way it developed was as optimum as could be.

GROVE: With all the Beatle activity that's going on today in the absence of The Beatles, themselves—the motion pictures, television specials, re-releases of their albums, the annual conventions of Beatle fans, the books and magazines, etc.—why do you think that all of this has come to a crest today in the late '70s?

SKLAR: First of all, because great art lives on. The creations live on. Nothing that great has come along to replace it. So there is a void, and the void is filled with the same material. Why do we keep having reruns of the old

139

Star Trek, for example?

GROVE: So in effect the need to resurrect The Beatles does not speak well for the state of the music industry today?

SKLAR: Nobody has come along to be their equal.

GROVE: Is there anybody you would say has come close?

SKLAR: Nope.

GROVE: Not even by a long shot?

SKLAR: Nope.

GROVE: The one name that I have heard mentioned from time to time as being perhaps the superstar of the '70s is Elton John.

SKLAR: Well, a great many stars are very popular and very big, but they're not as all-encompassing as The Beatles were.

GROVE: Is it more likely that the super recording star of the '70s would be an individual or a group?

SKLAR: It's hard to say.

GROVE: Was there something about the '60s that resulted in most of the recording acts then being groups? In the '70s it seems to me, we're seeing a lot more individual artists.

SKLAR: I think you're right.

GROVE: What, if anything, accounts for that?

SKLAR: Probably the finances of the music business. It's much more advantageous for people to make money as individuals. As soon as there's a group you have to split up the income that comes in from the same record or album that an individual would otherwise have.

GROVE: In conclusion, Rick, let me ask you where you see The Beatles going from here. We're now at a point about seven years after their split. They're still all young men. Hopefully, they'll live many, many years. Where do you see them in 1980 as individuals? What do you think will happen to them?

SKLAR: I know where I'd like to see them in 1980.

GROVE: Where is that?

SKLAR: I really would like to see them together. It's my sense of history. It's a certain hope that they would have an appreciation individually of their place in history that would lead them to the same conclusion.

GROVE: Perhaps to inevitably draw them back together again.

SKLAR: I think that at some point that might be an overriding consideration, when everything else has passed. At some point in their lives their place in history will become the most important factor to them.

GROVE: In effect, then, they would be saying, "we've had our fling, we've expressed our individuality, we've become known as individual artists...

SKLAR: ...and now let's grow up and be The Beatles again!"

XI

MOTION PICTURE STARS

The Beatles made their mark as musicians. Their albums sold more than 85 million and their singles topped 120 million.

Those statistics would tend to let people believe that The Beatles were musicians.

Not so.

They also were composers, lyricists, recording artists—three quitar players and a drummer.

But the Beatles were also motion picture players. Very active as actors in a thirty-seven sequence of films that was launched in 1964 with *A Hard Day's Night* that culminated in 1968 with *Yellow Submarine*.

The filmography that follows was prepared by Martin A. Grove, the noted author, with the assistance and cooperation of the library staff of the Academy of Motion Picture Arts & Sciences in Beverly Hills, California. They made their files readily available and provided Grove with a quickly produced set of Xerox copies of the reviews, articles, and credit sheets used to put together this filmography.

The filmography includes full details on The Beatles' activities in motion pictures and television films, with listings of casts and production credits where available. As presented in chronological order, the following alphabetical directory should be helpful to readers seeking information about a specific picture.

(a) *The Beatles On Film A To (Not Quite) Z.*

(1) Apotheosis (*John & Yoko*) - 1969

(2) Ballad of John & Yoko, The (*John & Yoko*) 1971

(3) Beatles At Shea Stadium, The (BBC-TV) 1966

(4) Blindman (*Ringo*) - 1971

(5) Born To Boogaloo (*directed by Ringo*) 1971

(6)   Candy (*Ringo*) - 1968
(7)   Cold Turkey (*John & Yoko*) - 1971
(8)   Concert For Bangla Desh, The (*George*) 1972
(9)   Erection (*John & Yoko*) - 1969
(10) Family Way, The (*music by Paul*) - 1966
(11) Fly *(John & Yoko)* - 1969
(12) Give Peace A Chance (*John & Yoko*)- 1971
(13) Hard Day's Night, A - 1964
(14) Help! - 1965
(15) Honeymoon (*John & Yoko*) - 1969
(16) How I Won The War (*John*) - 1967
(17) I Want To Hold Your Hand (*about Beatles*)
(18) Imagine (*John & Yoko*) - 1972
(19) Instant Karma (*John & Yoko*) - 1971
(20) Let It Be - 1969
(21) Lisztomania (*Ringo*) - 1975
(22) Little Malcolm And His Struggle Against The Eunuchs (*Executive Producer: George*) - 1974
(23) Live And Let Die (*title music by Paul*) - 1973
(24) Magic Christian, The (*Ringo*) - 1969
(25) Magical Mystery Tour (BBC-TV) - 1967
(26) Raga (*George*) - 1971
(27) Rape—Part II (*John & Yoko*) - 1969
(28) Self Portrait (*John & Yoko*) - 1969
(29) Sgt. Pepper's Lonely Hearts Club Band (*about Beatles*) - 1978
(30) Smile (*John & Yoko*) - 1969
(31) Son Of Dracula (*Produced by and starring Ringo*) - 1974
(32) That'll Be The Day (*Ringo*) - 1973
(33) 200 Motels (*Ringo*) - 1971
(34) Two Virgins *(John & Yoko)* - 1969
(35) Up Your Legs *(John & Yoko)* - 1971
(36) Wonderwall (*music by George*) - 1969
(37) Yellow Submarine (*animated Beatles*) - 1968

(b)*The Beatles on Film From 1964-78*

Death of a Dream

(1) *A Hard Day's Night* - A United Artists Release. Produced by Walter Shenson. Directed by Richard Lester. Screenplay by Alun Owen. Photography: Gilbert Taylor. Sound: H.L. Bird and Stephen Dalby. Film editor: John Jympson. Art direction: Ray Simm. Associate producer: Denis O'Dell. Assistant director: John D. Merriman. Music director: George Martin. Songs by John Lennon and Paul McCartney. Filmed in black & white. World première: July 6, 1964 at the Pavilion Theatre, London. Running time: 85 minutes.

Cast: John Lennon, Paul McCartney, George Harrison, Ringo Starr, Wilfrid Brambell, Derek Guyler, Kenneth Haigh, Norman Rossington, John Junkin, Richard Vernon, Anna Quayle and Victor Spinetti.

Reviews: In general, *A Hard Day's Night* was very well received by the critics, many of whom confessed that they were surprised that they had liked it. *Variety's* reviewer *Rich.* noted (7/14/64) that, "The Beatles appear to have it made in feature film circles, too." He said that *yeah, yeah, yeah* was the answer to questions about whether the group had a future performing. Like many film critics, he compared them to the Marx Brothers, suggesting that, "Carefully handled they well may develop the kind of cinematic zaniness that has not been seen since the Marx Brothers in their prime."

Calling them "potentially fine entertainers," he wrote that their first album "will satisfy the legion of Beatles' followers and should make the Group a lot of new friends who have sensed that there must be more behind them than the vocal twanging which has brought them such swift fame (notoriety ?) and fortune."

Al Finestone reviewed the picture for *The Hollywood Reporter* (7/21/64) and noted that, "The shrieking, screaming teenage reaction was evident at a packed invitational afternoon screening at a New York upper Broadway theatre. The mere appearance of a Beatle set off a chain reaction of screeching. When this mingled

145

with the screams of pursuing teenagers on the screen, the result was pandemonium."

Many of the reviewers and other VIPs who received screening invitations from United Artists had passed them along to their teenage sons and daughters. At that point in time, The Beatles were strictly a teenage attraction, and adults who didn't have to sit through the picture to write a review of it were only too happy to bestow their tickets on kids who were hung up on the mopheads. The result was a film screening that was every bit as noisey as actual Beatle performances at places like Carnegie Hall had been.

The *Reporter* also pointed out that the picture "is mad, mad and crazy, shrewdly designed for the teenage and calculated also to attract the curious and the oldsters who enjoy this sort of thing." Ringo was credited for showing "potential as a mime" in one sequence.

Writing in *Life* (8/7/64), Constantine FitzGibbon found himself "ready to agree that their fantastic appeal makes sense. In the first place they are sweet and endearing; secondly they are masculine and virile, and their singing packs a punch reminiscent of Maurice Chevalier at his best; in the third place they are healthy and funny and they don't give a damn for prejuices of their elders." He went on to note that the picture contained "a little elementary Marx Brothers surrealism." He concluded that, "It is a sort of cinemaverite with a tremendous amount of noise."

He made the additional point that the difference between the previous adulation for Elvis Presley or Frank Sinatra and that on The Beatles' behalf was that the first "was directly sexual," while the second "is all public, it is all mass emotion.... Indeed the emotion they inspire may be likened to that which girls used to feel when the soldiers came marching through the town, bands playing and flags flying."

Louis Pelegrine reviewed the picture for *The Film*

Daily (7/16/64), deciding that "United Artists has on its hands one heck of a hot commercial property." He added that, "Ample evidence to bear out this judgment was provided by the frenzied reaction of a teenage audience to the shraggy quartet's screen antics at a showing of the film at the Beacon Theatre in Manhattan."

Turning his critical eye to the matter, he wrote, "That the picture is inordinately noisy, shot through with confusion, weak in story, acted shoddily and burdened with questionable sound recording that makes much of the dialogue difficult to catch is unlikely to work to its detriment one iota." What mattered, he said, was that it "gives the kids their fill of Beatlemania. And that is all they are interested in."

Newsweek (8/24/64) declared that "the legitimacy of the Beatles phenomenon is finally inescapable." Its film critic decided that the film "does admirably well, mainly by being daring and fresh." Despite "the meagerest possible plot line," the result was called "a truly fresh, lively length of film."

"Of course the Beatles sing a lot, and shake their heads and wave their hair around," the review concluded, "but there is a sardonic edge to the film—as there is, generally, to the Beatles' style—which makes it surprisingly palatable, yeah, yeah, yeah."

Philip K. Scheuer, motion picture editor at the time for The Los Angeles *Times*, confessed (8/13/64) that, "The main surprise, at least to a square like me, is that the Beatles not only aren't monsters, they aren't even faintly grotty (grotesque). And while their sense of humor is unabashedly zany, there's an underlying gentleness...about their behavior which is hard to resist."

He also observed that, "the squeals of the girls—on-screen as well as off—all but drown them out anyway." Apparently, it was not only in New York City that Beatle fans in the audience found it impossible to refrain from shrieking.

Comparing The Beatles to Mac Sennett in terms of "visual gags," and to the Marx Brothers for "verbal" humor, he advised that "spontaneity is the keynote of the picture's technique, which has been shot a la New Wave in documentary or newsreel style."

A similar discovery that The Beatles were not the Devil incarnate was made by Harrison Carroll in the Los Angeles *Herald-Examiner* (8/13/64). Crediting the film for having "tremendous animation," he wrote "I had expected to find them a bore. To the contrary, I found them amusing, engaging."

Bosley Crowther, film critic at the time for The New York *Times*, wrote (8/16/64) that *A Hard Day's Night* "is a joyous reminder of the sort of fun the Marx Brothers used to spread, done up in the cluttered climate of the television age." He indicated that the picture "bids fair to be the most sensational commercial screen success of the year," and called The Beatles "likeable participants."

In his view, "is is, indeed, superb direction that helps to make the Beatles' film the rapid-fire, rollicking, good-humored and sophisticated spoof it is."

He noted that, "The British directors are getting remarkable effects with their cameras these days—bold and exciting rhythms and propulsive narrative leaps, combined with sharp and natural settings, that seem to catch the mood and tempo of the age."

Arthur Knight of the *Saturday Review* didn't catch up with *A Hard Day's Night* until a month late. In his review (9/19/64) he apologized for being so late in focusing on The Beatles, but explained "such phenomena are generally 'packaged' in a sleazy, indifferntly made exploitation picture that goes into hundreds of theatres simultaneously, on what is known as a saturation booking, so that the producers can get their money out of it before the public learns that it is being robbed. Since everything about A Hard Day's Night—posters, advertising, mass bookings—suggested just such a picture, I skipped the press screening. I was wrong."

Now having caught the film, he advised that The Beatles "have a neat sense of knockabout comedy timing that places them somewhere between the three Marx Brothers and the Three Stooges."

As for the direction by Richard Lester, he likened it to the "swift, elliptical, intimate style of Godard's *Breathless*" combined with the "wild, free-ranging, almost free-association approach of Phillippe de Broca."

He confessed to still being "mystified at the intensity of the furore these four amiable young men have stirred in the breasts of teenagers everywhere and suspect that some adroit pressagentry lies at the bottom of much of it." And he concluded that "by the time it is over, one feels he knows the boys—or at least hopes that they really are as unpretentious, fun-loving and direct as their picture makes them out to be."

Writing in *Film News* in 1975 (Vol. 32, No. 5) Ruth M. Goldstein looked back at *A Hard Day's Night* from the perspective of the '70s, years after The Beatles split up. She noted that, "In addition to the fun of Mack Sennett sight gags, Marx Brothers dialogue, fast cutting, and clever improvisation with a hand-held camera, *A Hard Day's Night* offers a glimpse of Beatlemania at its height—a social phenomenon of our immediate past, interesting to compare with current youth cults."

She observed that "one does not even have to be a Beatles' music fan to enjoy it," and was particularly taken by the "engaging qualities of the young men themselves."

In conclusion, she wrote, "It is not a bit hard to see why Beatlemania grew. Today's students can finish the story, for they know a great deal about what changed the Beatle music and the Beatles themselves, which cults of the Seventies are like and unlike that one."

When *A Hard Day's Night* was in production producer Walter Shenson was interviewed in London by Stephen Watts for an article in The New York *Times* (4/26/64).

He explained that the picture then being made "isn't an Elvis Presley fairy tale. The boys sing only when the story requires them to be seen in performance." He went on to discuss some of the self-imposed ground rules for making the picture.

The first was that there could be no Beatle romances. "I'd be torn apart by those fans, probably deported if one of the boys got mixed up with a girl," Mr. Shenson declared. A second restriction was that since The Beatles were instantly recognizable in real life, they had to be equally recognizable in the picture. In other words, they couldn't play roles in which people wouldn't know they were The Beatles. Finally, there had to be individual scenes for each of The Beatles to satisfy the groups of fans that had centered on each of them at the time. Moreover, Mr. Shenson indicated to the reporter that he had wanted to point up the fact that the four Beatles all had their own particular personalities.

The Beatles, themselves proposed Alun Owen to write the screenplay for *A Hard Day's Night*. It turned out to be a fictionalized account of 36 hours in the life of The Beatles. The suggestion of Richard Lester to direct was made by Mr. Shenson and, reportedly, was at first turned down by The Beatles. When they were told that Mr. Lester had been the director of the early Peter Sellers short *The Running, Jumping and Standing Still Film* they reversed themselves immediately and are said to have replied, "Get him."

The picture had its world premiere—a Royal Premiere, at that—in London on July 6, 1964. A crowd of 20,000 Beatle fans turned out in Piccadilly Circus in the vicinity of the London Pavilion Theatre. Some 500 policemen were on hand to control the crowds.

Also present were fifty members of the St. John's Ambulance Brigade, who devoted themselves to treating victims of hysteria as well as people who had been crushed against the metal fences that line the streets of that part of London.

There were 1200 people inside the London Pavilion for the movie's premiere, including Princess Margaret and her husband the Earl of Snowdon. It was reported at the time that when they arrived in front of the cinema "they received a loud cheer—but nothing like the Beatles had received."

Walter Shenson, was interviewed by Charles Champlin, entertainment editor of The Los Angles *Times*, for a story that ran on April 5, 1974. In it Mr. Shenson recalled the time of *A Hard Day's Night*. He asked, "Can you remember the craziness of those days? The adults were talking about '*those* boys' as if they were a threat to humanity. And that long hair, carefully shampooed. It doesn't even look long now."

Discussing the economics of the film, he said that United Artists "were going to put up $600,000 and they figured that whatever they lost on the movie they would make on the album. And as a matter of fact, the advance sale on the album were $600,000." As things turned out, UA's stake in the picture was reportedly about $750,000. The company is said to have realized a return of some $14 million! Although more money was spent on The Beatles' second film, *Help!*, the investment of a reported $1.25 million is said to have brought in about the same $14 million.

(2) *Help*—A United Artists release. Produced by Walter Shenson. Directed by Richard Lester. Screenplay by Marc Behm and Charles Wood, based on an original story by Marc Behm. Photography: David Watkin. Sound: Richard Bird. Film Editor: John Victor Smith. Art direction: Ken Thorne. Songs by John Lennon & Paul McCartney and George Harrison. Filmed in Eastmancolor. World premiere: July 29, 1965 at the Pavilion Theatre, London. Running time: 92 minutes.

Cast: John Lennon, Paul McCartney, George Harrison, Ringo Starr, Leo McKern, Eleanor Bron, Victor Spinetti, Roy Kinnear, Patrick Cargill, John Bluthal, Alfie Bass, Warren Mitchell, Peter Copley and Bruce Lacey.

Reviews: *Help!* was generally well received by the critics, many of whom compared it to *A Hard Day's Night*. While there seemed to have been more critical affection for the earlier picture, *Help!* was recognized to be different because of its storyline which put The Beatles through all sorts of fictional paces that hadn't interfered with them being themselves in their first film.

Writing in the *Motion Picture Herald* (8/18/65) Sy Oshinsky commented, *"Help!* isn't likely to be the cry coming from exhibitors showing this second picture by The Beatles, unless they find the crowds too large and enthusiastic to handle. All the successful ingredients poured into their first film, *A Hard Day's Night*, are in this production. Most important, of course, is the presence of The Beatles."

Like many other reviewers, he went on to note that "what *A Hard Day's Night* didn't have, and which *Help!* makes striking use of, is color photography."

He concluded that *Help!* "may seem a bit far fetched, but it has been produced with such zest and imagination that it comes off as high comedy."

In his review in *The Hollywood Reporter* (8/3/65) James Powers observed that the picture "is going to be a big, big, big hit, and United Artists is the happy distributor." He called it "a rocketing successor" to *A Hard Day's Night*, tempering that somewhat by adding that it "is not quite so thoroughly delightful as the first, but it is good enough: 'twill serve."

He, too, made mention of the benefit of the color photography, labeling it "the first time the Beatles have come across in their own glorious pallor."

Reflecting on why The Beatles were able to appeal to both young and old moviegoers, he decided it was because "they do what they do with grace and humor. Most of the many groups that have aped their bushy bobs, their sound and their songs, have neither. These boys give the impression that what they are doing is a great joke. They don't make fun of themselves. That would be unprofessional. But they perform their songs with such jolly good humor that it would take a very pompous type to resist them."

"In *Variety* (8/4/65) reviewer *Rich* announced that *Help!* "is bound to be a resounding boxoffice click. It is peppered with bright gags and situations and throwaway nonsense." He applauded Richard Lester for "expectedly alert" direction and called the use of color "a delight."

On the negative side, he spoke of "some frantically contrived spots and sequences that flag badly. The simple good spirits that pervaded *A Hard Day's Night* are now often smothered..."

Again reference was made to the Marx Brothers, with the comment that the story, itself, "would have been a useful Marx Bros. vehicle." As for the songs, they "do nothing to help along the plot or situations but are agreeable for Beatles' fans..."

On the performing side, he found that "The Beatles prove more relaxed in front of the camera at this, their second attempt, and many of their throwaway gags are choice non sequiturs....They have still to prove themselves to be actors, but as screen personalities they are good material and have a touch of the Marx Bros. in their similar irreverent flights of fantasy."

What about their future in motion pictures? Noting that it "is still not possible to assess," he conceded that "They are moneyspinners, but how they will develop as artists is a riddle. Perhaps their third will find a happy medium between the explosive anarchy and novelty of their first and the more conventional slapstick fun and games of this new offering."

The action of *Help!* differed greatly from the near-documentary approach of *A Hard Day's Night*. In *Help!* the plot concerned a ring worn by (naturally) Ringo. The ring turns out to be the sacred symbol of some Eastern cult, which wants it back. Hence, the chase! The cult pursues Ringo—and his three pals, of course—to such picturesque locales as the Bahamas, the Austrian Alps, the Salisbury Plains and Buckingham Palace, itself! Other than the fact that The Beatles are identified as The Beatles, everything else in *Help!* is sheer fiction. In *A Hard Day's Night*, there was some fictionalization—such as the invention of a mischievous old grandfather for Paul—but the action was essentially correct. In real life, 36 hours with The Beatles could have looked the way it was shown on the screen.

Not everyone liked *Help!* Dale Munroe of the Hollywood *Citizen News* complained (8/31/65) that "the trouble with *Help!* is that it is confused, disjointed, badly edited venture—more nearly akin to an unrelated bunch of satirically produced TV sight-gag-type commercials loosely strung together in order to fill the required feature length running time, than to a properly conceived motion picture—in any sense of that word."

He added, however, that "on the credit side for Beatle fans (who incidentally did not indulge in the screaming expected of them during the preview screening) is the performance of seven new Beatle songs written especially for the film..."

The author's own recollection of the screening he attended at the time in New York City is that there was far less screaming in the audience there, too. This is probably because many of those persons who had given away their invitations to *A Hard Day's Night* the previous year now realized that The Beatles' films were fun. They kept the tickets for themselves when *Help!* came along. Naturally, the older moviegoers showed considerably more restraint than their teenage sons and daughters had.

Bosley Crowther wrote in The New York *Times* (8/29/65) that *Help!* was "a lively, funny picture," but he noted that "it hasn't the wit or substance of the Beatles' first film..." In his view, *Help!* misses the winsomeness and freshness of that cheerful, forthright kidding of themselves..."

On the plus side, though, he found that "it does have a friendly, wholesome spirit, a delight in absurdity and the youthful exuberance and musical fervor of the famous mop-headed rock 'n' roll quartet."

Mr. Crowther addressed himself to the comparisons that had been made of The Beatles and The Marx Brothers. He explained that "each of the comical Marxes was a significant caricature...The Beatles, for all their freshness and their good, clean boyish charm, have not yet discovered and developed distinctive comic characters." He thought Ringo came closest as "the sad sack, the butt of the jokes," but called the others "just happy, glib young chaps who toss off lines and get a kick out of living, singing and doing zany things."

Summing things up, he labeled *Help!* "surrealistic slapstick or a cinema happening. It is pop art put into motion and joyously travested. It is a fun thing that mirrors the irreverence and uninhibitedness of youth."

He concluded that, "It conforms to a culture and taste that have been nourished by rock 'n' roll singers, comic strips, the Three Stooges, James Bond, science-fiction movies and elephant jokes."

"Lowell E. Redelings was more enthusiastic in his review in the Los Angeles *Herald-Examiner* (9/2/65). He called *Help!* "a weird picture—sort of a takeoff on the wild shenanigans of the Pearl White silent film serials, plus modern-day gadget weapons." Although he found the film "jerky in spots; some of the transitions are too abrupt, possibly due to cutting of footage, and a few sequences confusing, storywise," he decided that "it's a brisk, picturesque and largely amusing comedy." He found the use of color "most commendable."

In conclusion, he declared "it's a capital B everywhere for the Beatles, like in Boxoffice."

Generally, *Help!* came off less well than *A Hard Day's Night* in comparisons of the two pictures by the critics.

For instance, *The New Yorker's* review (8/28/65) noted that *"Help!* isn't quite such an effortless-seeming feat of spontaneous combustion as *A Hard Day's Night,"* but agreed that "it's still wonderful enough for all impractical purposes."

The magazine also observed that, "In the Beatles' first picture, the pretense was made that we were being treated to a fairly accurate account of their usual terrestrial activities...In *Help!* several hands have cobbled up a screenplay of wholly unnecessary complexity, in which, while the Beatles remain themselves, everything else is fantasy—a simultaneous plundering of the works of Sax Rohmer, Edgar Wallace, Rider Haggard, and S.J. Perelman."

Kenneth Tynan's review of *Help!* in the London *Observer* was reprinted in the Los Angeles *Times* on August 11, 1965. He cited *Help!* as being "a brilliant, unboring but ferociously ephemeral movie."

He found the direction by Richard Lester to be "a high-speed compendium of many lessons learned from Blake Edwards, Frank Tashlin, good comedy, fashion photography and MGM cartoons."

Turning to The Beatles as performers, he allowed that although they "are not natural actors, nor are they exuberant extroberts, their mode is dry and laconic, as befits the flat and skeptical Liverpool accent." He also singled out the musical scenes as being "superbly shot, and the title song is the most haunting Beatle composition to date."

The Los Angeles *Times'* motion picture editor, Philip K. Scheuer, called *Help!* "a nutty film and sometimes an inspired one..." He seemed to like it more than *A Hard Day's Night,* commenting that "The new picture is even funnier and more Marx-like than *A Hard Day's Night.* I have heard criticism that it is neither as wistful nor 'poetic' and I am not disposed to argue, though neither do I care very much."

In appraising The Beatles as actors, he noted that they "are strange young men, but also likable. They aren't really actors but in all this razzmatazz, who's to notice?"

He concluded that, *Help!* "is shot as informally as a home movie, with the camera and sound track jumping when the boys are not, and the wise person will not try to analyze it, let alone rationalize it. The point is that it made me laugh."

Hollis Alpert of the *Saturday Review* (8/28/65) wasn't greatly impressed by *Help!* He pointed out that, "the fuzz is off the peach, so to speak. I didn't find the Beatles nearly as cute, funny or diverting this time. The spontaneity is forced, and the humor reminded me much more of the old Abbott and Costello movies than of the Marx Brothers, to whom they were given the honor of being compared last time out."

Mr. Alpert reassured his readers, "I'm not really worried about Beatles and never was. But I *am* worried about Richard Lester, an immensely talented director. I think he needs to get away from Beatles for a while. Is it my imagination, or do I hear him faintly in the distance crying 'help!' All the way to the bank, of course."

The *New Republic's* critic noted (9/25/65) that "the chief problem of the second film, called *Help!*, is that the first one has been made. Luxuriation in the existence and resonances of Beatle-facts could not suffice a second time; a plot had to be used. Thus, almost automatically, this relegated the new film to a somewhat lesser place."

That seems to be a particularly relevant point. No matter what The Beatles did as their second film it would always have been *second* and, therefore, lacking the initial impact and newness of whatever had come *first*.

Nonetheless, the magazine found that "The Beatles are no less likeable than ever and still very lucky in their director."

George Harrison was interviewed by Robin Bean for an article about *Help!* in the July 1965 edition of the

British magazine *Films and Filming*. "We just wouldn't have made a film ever if we had made a film like the usual thing," the Beatle explained. "We had a lot of offers for the thing where the group's playing at the high school dance and that sort of rubbish and we just didn't want to know."

He added that, "Then Walter and Dick came along who were as much with us on this; they wanted it to be our film and nothing to do with all this dancing on a beach and all that crap."

George was also quoted as saying, "We had a lot of trouble with this one, just trying to think of ways of how to get a song into the film, because let's face it it's got to have songs in it because it's us, and we wouldn't be here but for our songs. So we have to think of feasible ways of putting a song in without it looking corny...."

Indicating something of the control The Beatles were not able to exercise over their motion picture material, George explained, "If there's something in the script that we'd never say in a month of Sundays we'll just ask Dick to change it; it's pointless seeing that it is supposed to be us."

At the time of the interview The Beatles were apparently planning to do a Western based on the book *A Talent For Loving* as their third picture. The novel by Richard Condon had originally been planned as a vehicle for Peter Sellers and Peter Ustinov.

"Richard Condon's already written the script," George went on. "The main heart of the book is the second half, he has just taken odd little bits from the second half. He's enlarged the two main characters into four for us, and the only other person we need is a strong actor for the part of the major. We'd like to get somebody like Peter Sellers, he'd be great."

What about the problem of The Beatles' Liverpool accents in the American Old West? "The thing with this is that it is a feasible situation for us to get into because it's

Sheila Hancock, Charles Dyer, Bill Dysart, Paul Daneman, Peter Graves, Jack May, Richard Pearson, Pauline Taylor, John Ronane, Norman Chappell, Bryan Pringle, Fanny Carby, Dandy Nichols, Gretchen Franklin, John Junkin, John Trenaman, Mick Dillon and Kenneth Colley.

Reviews: A quick look at the credits associated with *How I Won The War* suggests that it was only natural for John Lennon to associate himself with the project. Many of the people had worked with The Beatles before. Richard Lester, of course, directed both *A Hard Day's Night* and *Help!* Charles Wood had been a co-author of the *Help!* screenplay. David Watkin had photographed *Help!* John Victor Smith was the film editor for *Help!* And UA had released both Beatles pictures.

Reviewing the film for *Variety* (10/25/67) *Murf* tagged it "an uneven, forced black comedy in which liabilities outweigh assets. John ("The Beatles") Lennon has some marquee value, but his part is small." He further noted that "Lennon, whose billing far exceeds his part, and contribution, plays one of the crew."

He also found that, "A prominent flaw which inhibits pic in incomprehensible dialog; the cockney slang may be authentic in content and delivery, in which case film may kill 'em in London nabes (neighborhood theatres). Rest of the world is something else again. But, judging from what can be understood (sound recording, incidentally, is crisp, therefore presumably blameless), nothing much is missed."

The Hollywood Reporter's John Mahoney (10/24/67) wrote that, "There are flashes of brilliance, telling moments which give way to the torpor of largely unintelligible interstices." He explained that, "The presence of John Lennon in a minor, ill-defined role provides further insurance and curiosity."

He also observed that, "Lennon wanders in and out physically as well as verbally, saying some clever things, mumbling other things, inciting interest by virtue of personality, but without ever having his interest in the film complemented by substance in the script."

In *Our Sunday Visitor* (11/5/67) John E. Fitzgerald stated that "no doubt Lennon's appearance will have a calculated emotional effect on young audiences." He told his readers that the movie "stars, despite publicity, not John Lennon, whose role is actually quite minor, but Michael Crawford..." But he did concede that "Since The Beatles are no strangers to our country, Lennon's appeal is enormous."

Penelope Mortimer reviewed *How I Won The War* for the London *Observer* (10/22/67) and began by saying that Richard Lester "plays tricks on us. First, there is the star billing of John Lennon; Mr. Lennon appears very infrequently, in light disguise, and while his Liverpudlian accents are as endearing and earth-bound as ever, his acting suffers in comparison with pros such as Roy Kinnear, Lee Montague and Jack MacGowran." Another trick, in her opinion, was presenting the picture "as a riot, a rib-tickling fun-packed romp." It was, instead, in Ms. Mortimer's view, "the dourest and sourest picture I have seen since *Dr. Strangelove*."

She concluded by noting that, "I am told that this film will not be shown on the circuits (theatre chains in England), and the reason seems fairly clear. It is too uncomfortable, in spite of Mr. Lennon."

Mr. Lester went on the record once as saying, "I believe I have made a genuinely pacifist film. It is an anti-war film, of course, but is also a film against war films. I wanted to show war without kicks, the opposite of the conventional tank opera. There is no single statement in it that I do not believe to be to the right purpose. I am totally responsible and, if it has gone wrong, there is only me to blame. But if I fell under a bus tomorrow, this is the film I'd want to be judged by."

Analysis of a variety of reviews of *How I Won The War*

indicates that many film critics felt the picture fell short of greatness, and thought Mr. Lester's earlier efforts with The Beatles would represent a greater monument to his career in the cinema.

As for John Lennon's debut in a straight dramatic role, virtually all the reviewers made note of the event. It appears that most critics thought he handled his acting chores pretty well. In *Esquire's* review (January 1968), for instance, a closing parenthetical reference was made to John — "Incidentally, to answer the second question everyone asks: John Lennon is adequate."

In an interview with Jean Antel for The New York *Times* whle the picture was being filmed, John Lennon had confided, "I didn't know what filmmaking was all about, really. This has given me the chance to see it from the inside. In the Beatle films we were just—I don't know—they were wrong somehow. We are just playing our old parts."

He had gone on to say, "we can't make any more Beatle films. That's certain. And we don't really want to become film actors. I suppose we don't know what we want to do. Individually, I mean. Or apart from what we do as Beatles. Oh yes, we'll go on with *that*. Of course, any one of us might take on some acting role in the future. It all depends on the role...."

Asked why John Lennon, with no previous experience as a dramatic actor, had been selected for his movie, Richard Lester told the interviewer, "I have a very high regard for the Beatles. It just happens that we thought this part was something that John would enjoy doing, and that he could do well. I consider Lennon an extraordinarily intelligent man. I don't mean that lightly. I've known perhaps two or three people in a lifetime who could compare with him in intelligence. Furthermore, he's a born entertainer. All this highly qualifies him as an actor. And if he wishes to act, of course, he's bound to get better. He could be a very fine actor if he's willing to go ahead. It's a question of practice and willingness."

(6) *MAGICAL MYSTERY TOUR* — An Apple Production for BBC-TV in England. Produced, directed and written by The Beatles. Photography: Richard Starkey, M.B.E. (Ringo Starr, of course!). Songs by John Lennon & Paul McCartney and George Harrison. Filmed in color. World premiere: December 16, 1967 on BBC-1 network. Running time: originally 55 minutes but cut to 50 minutes for television.

Cast: John Lennon, Paul McCartney, George Harrison, Ringo Starr, George Claydon, Jessie Robins, Ivor Cutler, Derek Royle, Shirley Evans, Victor Spinetti, Nat Jackley, Mandy Weet, Nicola and Maggie Wright.

Reviews: Magical Mystery Tour was The Beatles' first failure in five years. The television film was dismissed by British critics and audiences when it was presented by BBC-1 as part of its Christmas programming for 1967. Among the critial opinions hurled at The Beatles were such things as "tasteless nonsense," "blatant rubbish," and "a great big bore."

The *Daily Express* observed that, "The whole boring saga confirmed a long-held suspicion that the Beatles are four rather pleasant young men who have made so much money that they can apparently afford to be contemptuous of the public."

The program's failure was reported by newspapers around the world. Typical of the way the story was handled was this headline in the Los Angeles *Times* (12/18/67): "CRITICS AND VIEWERS BOO: BEATLES PRODUCE FIRST FLOP WITH YULE FILM." The story went on to quote Paul McCartney as admitting, "I suppose we goofed, really." But it also reported him as saying, "It is better to be controversial than purely boring."

According to the dispatch from London the bulk of complaints about *Magical Mystery Tour* related to its having "appeared amateurish" in comparison to The

Beatles' two earlier films, *A Hard Day's Night Help!*

Time (1/5/68) reported that the result of The Beatles' first efforts as their own producers, directors, and writers was "a disjointed series of day-dreams, nightmares, cloudscapes, reveries and slapstick skits."

The magazine credited Paul with having directed — although the official credits indicated only that The Beatles had produced, directed and written the program — and quoted him as saying, "We didn't worry about the fact that we didn't know anything about making films. We realized years ago you don't need knowledge in this world to do anything. All you need is sense, whatever that is."

As for the show's failure, *Time* quoted Paul's view that, "Aren't we entitled to have a flop? Was the film really so bad compared with the rest of the Christmas TV? You could hardly call the Queen's speech a gasser."

In conclusion, the newsweekly noted that failure or not, *Magical Mystery Tour* "will net the Beatles about $2,000,000" thanks to scheduled telecasts in other countries.

When originally shown in England on December 26, 1967 by BBC-1 the film was telecast in black & white. A second telecast, this time in color, was made on January 5, 1968 by BBC-2, which had color TV facilities at the time. Unfortunately, fewer British television sets were then equipped to receive the smaller BBC-2 network, so most viewers in England never saw *Magical Mystery Tour* in color.

Not everyone thought the film was a flop, however. *Variety's* reviewer *Mull.* wrote that the "opus has the air of the enthusiastic amateur about it. But herein lies much of its appeal, for there is something refreshing about an approach which allowed scenes to be devised, and dialog often improvised, as ideas occurred during the filming."

Discussing The Beatles as producers, he called it "obvious that their talent is not limited to music. Given an opportunity to acquire more technical expertise, they could easily triumph before long in the production medium."

As for *Magical Mystery Tour's* chances, *Mull.* predicted that, "Assumng, as promised, that technical problems, including uneven color balance and poor sound quality, evident in this rough-cut version, were licked in time for the BBC vidcast...the Beatles are on to another winner." And he found it "easy to ignore the faults in face of the sheer exuberance of the whole segment."

As things turned out at the time, some of the technical problems apparently weren't resolved prior to the telecast. Viewers and critics alike turned thumbs down on the project. *Variety's* enthusiasm seemed misplaced. On the other hand, from the perspective of today the tradepaper was probably right on the mark. Since 1967 *Magical Mystery Tour* has achieved cult status with Beatles' fans who have been able to see it in the United States.

The picture was screened in New York at the Fillmore East and in San Francisco at the Fillmore West, both of which were rock music halls, not cinemas. *Magical Mystery Tour* had its American movie theatre premiere at the Savoy Theatre in Boston from December 17 to 24, 1968. That was approximately one year after its first telecast on BBC-1.

Ben Blumenberg reviewed the film in *Boston After Dark* (12/18/68) under the headline "BEATLES PROVE MAGICAL IN 'MYSTERY TOUR' MOVIE." He found that "the great success of the film is the great success of the Beatles as human beings." He added that the "film demonstrates in the most complete fashion to date what all of us Beatles' fans knew anyway. That is that their complexity and many-leveled approach should be applicable to any form."

Comparing it to *Yellow Submarine*, which actually

followed it by some seven months but arrived in the U.S. ahead of it, he wrote that, "any one form (music) should be able to provide the basis for any other (visuals). *Magical Mystery Tour* is a more complete demonstration of this than *Yellow Submarine* because (1) it is solely an Apple creation, and (2) the music is the skeleton for the photography. In *Yellow Submarine*, one song led to a story that became the framework for the entire film."

In conclusion, Mr. Blumenberg called the picture "complex, lyrical and at times surprisingly sobering, but always fun."

From time to time *Magical Mystery Tour* has popped up throughout the the United States. In mid-May 1968 it had four showings in Los Angeles at the Los Feliz Theatre and two showings at the Esquire Theatre in Pasadena. It had two showings on one evening in the spring of 1975 at the Nuart Theatre in Los Angeles, along with several other hard-to-find films by individual Beatles. A promotional piece by the theatre noted that it would be screening "a complete, fantastic print of *Magical Mystery Tour* (most prints of the latter have been in extremely bad shape)."

Plans for *Magical Mystery Tour* had originally been announced in September 1967. The Beatles had been planning to do a television special based on their *Sgt. Pepper's Lonely Hearts Club Band* album, according to reports at the time. But, instead, they decided to create *Magical Mystery Tour*. To undertake the project they postponed a trip to India that had been planned so as to get underway with filming.

After the film was completed it was reported that Geoffrey Ellis, managing director of Nems Enterprises, which then managed The Beatles' business affairs, was planning to visit New York in early January 1968 to put together an American television deal. No such telecast in the U.S. was ever arranged, most likely due to the poor reception the film received in Britain.

With today's revival of interest in The Beatles, there would no doubt be a substantial audience for *Magical Mystery Tour* it if were shown on American television.

There was not much plot involved in *Magical Mystery Tour*. The premise apparently was to fill a big yellow bus with The Beatles and some 39 other people and drive around the British countryside for a few weeks. As they undertook their unusual tour improvisation was the practice of the day. Dialogue was made up as filming took place. Scenes were created on the spot. It was a very different kind of filmmaking, and probably stands as an early companion to The Beatles' *Let It Be* film, which also was an uncharted and relatively unpolished work. Both projects seem to represent The Beatles' desire to get away from the basic techniques of polishing something over and over in the studio — of doing umpteen takes of a film scene or musical selection until it is totally and absolutely perfect.

(7) *CANDY* — A Cinerama Releasing Corp. release. A Christian Marquand production. Executive producers: Selig J. Seligman for Selmur Pictures; and Peter Zoref for Les Films Corona. Produced by Robert Haggiag for Dear Films. Directed by Christian Marquand. Screenplay by Buck Henry. Based on the novel by Terry Southern (under the pseudonym Maxwell Kenton) and Mason Hoffenberg. Photography: Giuseppe Rotunno. Film editors: Frank Santillo and Giancarlo Cappelli. Mucic: Dave Grusin. Art director: Dean Tavoularis. Sound: Mario Celebtano and Basil Fenton Smith. Assistant directors: Francesco Cinieri and Luciano Sacripanti. Title song performed by The Byrds. Additional songs: Steppenwolf. MPAA rating: R. Filmed in Technicolor. Running time: 123 minutes.

Cast: Charles Aznavour, Marlon Brando, Richard Burton, James Coburn, John Huston, Walter Matthau, Ringo Starr, Ewa Aulin, John Astin, Elsa Martinelli, Sugar Ray Robinson, Anita Pallenberg, Lea Padovani,

Florinda Bolkan, Marilu Tolo, Nicoletta Machiavelli, Umberto Orsini, Joey Forman, Fabian Dean and Enrico Maria Salerno.

Reviews: Ringo Starr made his solo debut as a film actor in *Candy*. In his *Daily Variety* review (12/17/68) *Murf.* observed that, "Ringo Starr, as the Mexican gardner who next falls as willing victim of Candy's wiles, is very good. As for the picture itself, he called it "a mixed bag of goodies," and added that "book's reputation will be a selling factor, also the camero players."

The Film and Television Daily (12/18/68) took an opposite view. Edward Lipton's review commented that, "Ringo Starr, as the Mexican gardner, is mostly wasted, but contributes his name for marquee value." He went on to say that, "Those who said that *Candy* could not be translated to the screen world, thus far, appear to have been essentially correct." He did, however, note that the "excellent" casting and the "pre-sell factor" would probably "stir up fine business at the box office."

(8) *YELLOW SUBMARINE* — A United Artists release. An Apple Films presentation. A King Features/Subafilms production. Produced by Al Brodax. Directed by George Dunning. Screenplay by Lee Minoff, Al Brodax, Jack Mendelsohn and Erich Segal. Original story by Lee Minoff, based on the song *Yellow Submarine* by John Lennon and Paul McCartney. Music by The Beatles. Musical diector: George Martin. Chief Designer: Heinz Edelman. Animation directors: Jack Stokes and Robert E. Balser. Special effects: Charles Jenkins. Production coordinator: Abe Goodman. Filmed in Color by DeLuxe. Running time: 87 minutes.

Cast: The Beatles (animated and, in a brief end sequence, live); and the voices of Dick Emery, Lance Percival, Paul Angelus and Sheila Danille.

Reviews: Although *Yellow Submarine* did not do terribly well at the box office, it was well received by the critics. Most reviewers contrasted its style of animation with the older and more traditional Disney style.

Disney's style of animation was based on the use of circles, which enabled his characters to move by rolling. This is easier to achieve than the movement of angular or rectangular forms. Producer Al Brodax was quoted in an interview as explaining, "The figures (in *Yellow Submarine*) are wildly distorted, thus difficult to move. Circles move easily; they roll. Rectangles just bump along. It took six weeks to devise a method to make them move and we were, at first, only partially successful. John, Paul and George finally began moving, but Ringo appeared to have a limp. It took another six weeks to adjust optics and modify drawings in order to get Ringo moving properly."

Daily Variety's reviewer, *Rich.,* predicted (7/23/68) that, "The pic should be a sure click with Beatles' fans and youthful 'pop' audiences and also intrigue those who sometimes tut-tut the remarkable combo's more wayout activities."

He added that, "George Martin, the Beatles' musical director, has done a smoothly elegant job with the cleffing and the songs come to life with visual verve as well as being easy on the ear."

In *The Hollywood Reporter* (7/23/68) John Mahoney wrote that, "Generally, the film captures the Beatles' style of punning humor and non-sequitur even more vitally than their live action features."

He commented that, "by assigning individual directors and animation units to a dozen Beatles' songs, which in effect comprise the plot of Yellow Submarine, the film acquires an exciting variety of visual textures and styles. It also gets stuck with no less than four anti-climaxes which make the latter portion of its brief 87 minutes painfully long and pretentiously cute, overplaying its own invention."

In his view, "George Martin's musical direction and

electronic wizardry is a marvel." He pointed out that, "It has been said that the British quartet do not speak their own dialogue in the film, but the aural likeness is so close that it is hard to believe."

Cue magazine (11/16/68) called the picture "delightful to watch," and said that "What distinguishes *Yellow Submarine*, with songs by the Beatles adding merriment to the charm of their cartoon likenesses, is a gloriously conceived mod look of the 1960s."

Renata Adler, movie critic at the time for The New York *Times*, observed (11/17/68) that, "It is a delicate, friendly, unpretenious film — which, if it did not have the imprimatur of the Beatles, with their special talent, power and grace would be of no great importance."

She also addressed herself to the picture's relationship (if any) to marijuana. "It is the perfect film, I think, for children, never terrifying, often funny, sometimes inspired and yet (or maybe, and so), there is the matter of pot," she wrote. "There is no question that *Yellow Submarine* (and a lot of totally undistinguished movies, like the Monkees' recent *Head*) are to a certain extent informed by marijuana, and that regardless of what its legal implications are, its esthetic importance is becoming more than marginal."

That same point was tackled by Richard Schickel in his *Life* magazine review of the movie. He commented that, "Some college kids have recently told me that the only way to appreciate Stanley Kubrick's *2001* fully is to go into the theater stoned and dig it as a light show. That may be so, but *Yellow Submarine* needs no such artificial flavoring. Indeed, it might very well blow a mind that approached it high."

To him, "the most important thing about *Yellow Submarine* needs no such artificial flavoring. Indeed, it might very well blow a mind that approached it high."

To him, "the most important thing about *Yellow Submarine* is its wondrous visual freedom. I suppose you could say its basic style is psychedelic."

He explained that, "What is unique about the Beatles is that they have standards: they did not accept just any old animation. Instead, they have put their name to a film that may rescue this great art form from the doldrums in which it has so long languished, at least in the West."

Les Schwartz reviewed the film for the Motion Picture *Herald* (10/30/68) and labeled it "something that is so far removed from just about anything anybody has ever done tht indescriable is the only way to describe it. There is so much happening in the turned-on world of *Yellow Submarine* that one can only smile from ear to ear and stare in wide-eyed wonder at the animated exploits of the four hip Britons."

He did point out that "actually, the Beatles themselves had little to do with the technical craftsmanship that distinguishes this film. But they provided the inspiration, the tone of humor, 11 songs (three new ones) and their all-important physical forms..."

Many of the critics addressed themselves to the style of art employed in the movie. The Los Angeles *Times'* Art Editor, Henry J. Seldis, reviewed the film (11/15/68) and said that it "adds up to a thoroughly Surrealistic experience not only through the recognizable graphic roots provided by De Chirico, Dali, Magritte and Ernst, but by its overabundance of visual and verbal puns." To him it was "the most stupendous animation feat in decades."

Time magazine (11/22/68) was in the minority in calling the film a "Bad Trip" in its headline. Its review complained that "the score includes several hits by the Beatles and just as many misses. The plot and the animation seem too square for hippies and too hip for squares."

In *Time's* view, "ultimately, however, what is wrong with the film is the Beatles. They are not in it. Except for the songs and a final sequence in which they appear live in some drab sing-along footage, they had nothing to do with *Yellow Submarine*. All but the most confirmed Beatlemaniacs can profit by their example."

Writing in *Films and Filming* David Rider pointed out that, "The Beatles themselves are beautifully designed and animated but their speaking voices are supplied by actors, who get remarkably close to the laconic, throwaway style exemplified in their live-action films."

He thought that "the virtues of *Yellow Submarine* far outweigh its vices of excessive length, occasional evidence of haste and an indecisive ending." In this view, "with the name of the Beatles attached to it, *Yellow Submarine* is at least assured of drawing the audiences into the cinemas."

The New Yorker's Pauline Kael agreed that while "The Beatles' non-singing voices are not their own...they're good." She wrote that The Beatles are "no longer the rebellious, anarchistic Pop idols that parents were at first so outraged by; they're no longer threatening. They're hippies as folk heroes, enshrined in our mythology."

She observed that the picture "uses Pop heroes and Pop Art deliberately, and with sophistication. And it works."

Charles Champlin, entertainment editor of the Los Angeles *Times*, reviewed the picture (11/15/68), finding that "there has come to seem no limit to the magic the Beatles can produce, or inspire others to produce."

He felt that "the impact and the pleasure of *Yellow Submarine* is still more visual than musical." In his opinion, "when the Beatles show up at the end in plain old photography to warn that the Blue Meanies are among us all the time, ready to pounce whenever we skimp on love or song, it's a plain old let-down and whoever would have thought it?"

(9) *WONDERWALL* — A Cinecenta Film Distributors release. Produced by Andrew Braunsberg for Alan Clore Films. Directed by Joe Massot.

Screenplay by G. Cain. Based on an original story by Gerard Brach. Music by George Harrison. Photography: Harry Waxman. Sound: Laurie Clarkson. Editor: Rusty Coppleman. Art Director: Asheton Gorton. Assistant Director: Jonathan Benson. Filmed in Eastmancolor. Running time: 94 minutes.

Cast: Jack MacGowran, Jane Birkin, Irene Handl, Richard Wattis, Iain Quarrier, Beatrix Lehmann, Brian Walsh, Sean Lynch and Bee Duffell.

Reviews: Those reviewers who made note of the fact that George Harrison composed the musical score for *Wonderwall* generally seemed to approve of what he did. In his *Variety* review (1/24/69) *Rich.* commented that the picture "has a score by Beatle George Harrison that cannot claim to be very tuneful, but has the right atmospheric style."

He thought the film "is a fairly rubbishy piece but it has a number of plusses which raises it from the utterly trivial." George's music was, apparently, one of those plusses.

Gordon Gow reviewed *Wonderwall* in *Films and Filming* (March 1969). He told his readers, "Unless you are jaded by too prolonged an exposure to the swinging half-myth, you might quite enjoy the blending of bright colours and Harrison music in *Wonderwall.*"

In a further note about the music, he wrote, "the Harrison music replaces dialogue, waxing almost vocal like a cinema organist from the silent days."

(10) *THE MAGIC CHRISTIAN* — A Commonwealth United presentation. Executive producers: Henry T. Weinstein and Anthony B. Unger. Produced by Denis O'Dell. Directed by Joseph McGrath. Screenplay by Terry Southern, Joseph McGrath and Peter Sellers. Based on the novel by Terry Southern. Music by Ken Thorne, Songs by Paul McCartney, Tom and Pete, Pete & Mike, John Keen and Noel Coward. Photography: Geoffrey Unsworth.

Production designer: Asheton Gorton. Film editor: Kevin Connor. Art director: George Djurkovic. Costume designer: Vangie Harrison. Choreography: Lionel Blair. Sound: Brian Holland. Special effects: Wally Veevers. Assistant director: Roger Simons. Filmed in Technicolor. Running time: 95 minutes.

Cast: Peter Sellers, Ringo Starr, Isabel Jeans, Caroline Blakiston, Wilfrid Hyde White, Richard Attenborough, Leonard Frey, Laurence Harvey, Christopher Lee, Spike Milligan, Roman Polanski, Raquel Welch, Tom Boyle, Terence Alexander, Peter Bayliss, Joan Benham, Patrick Cargill, Graham Chapman, John Cleese, Clive Dunn, Freddie Earle, Fred Emney, Kenneth Fortescue, Patrick Holt, Peter Graves, David Hutcheson, Hattie Jacques, John LeMesurier, Jeremy Lloyd, David Lodge, Victor Maddern, Ferdy Mayne, Guy Middletown, Peter Myers, Dennis Price, Robert Raglan, Graham Stark, Leon Thau, Frank Thornton, Michael Trubshawe, Edward Underdown, Michael Aspel, Michael Barratt, Harry Carpenter, W. Barrington Dalby, John Snagge and Alan Whicker.

Reviews: *The Magic Christian* marked Ringo Starr's second appearance on screen as an individual non-Beatle actor. Film critics seemed to generally view his role as relatively unimportant other than for the value of Ringo's name on the marquee.

In his *Variety* review (12/17/69) *Rich.* commented that, "Ringo Starr's second effect to project himself as a non-Beatle actor (he was in *Candy*) is a distinct non event."

He did note, however, that "there's some lively music and a half-dozen pleasant songs, including Paul McCartney's *Come And Get It*."

Time magazine (2/23/70) concluded that, "The only comic relief in the whole ghastly affair is created by Ringo — to no one's credit but his own. Director Joseph McGrath apparently intended to exploit the popular

Beatle brand of ironic mischief. Instead, Ringo's smirking indifference to his superfluous role neatly mocks the film itself."

In the Los Angeles *Herald-Examiner* (2/1/70) entertainment editor Winfred Blevins remarked, "Peter Sellers and Ringo Starr made it blithely witty and fun. Paul McCartney has written a song which drolly captures the movie's theme — *Come and Get It*, that is, come and snatch the money before it's gone."

She went on to say that, "Starr, making his debut in a major role, as a single, is given precious little to do except watch Sellers. He makes a good foil, but we will have to wait for another occasion to see fully what he is capable of."

Interestingly, despite the fact that Ringo's role was a small one he got the lion's share of the film's publicity. Both *Time* and the Los Angeles *Herald-Examiner* accompanied their reviews with pictures of Ringo and a scantily clad whip-wielding Raquel Welch. Other publications, too, selected photos of Ringo to illustrate their reviews of *The Magic Christian*. There's nothing wrong with this, but some readers might have found it misleading when they saw the film and discovered that Ringo had "precious little to do," as Ms. Belvins put it.

(11) *FILMS OF JOHN & YOKO* — John Lennon and Yoko Ono have produced, directed written and appeared in a number of short films over the years. These are rather obscure pictures today, but they have received occasional showings in the United States and abroad. In 1969, for instance, John & Yoko's *Rape—Part II* was shown in Germany at the Mannheim Film Festival during International Film Week (November 6-11). The 75-minute movie had previously been telecast in Austria. Its title is something of a misnomer since there is no rape in the conventional sense. The rape is done by camera only. The subject of this rape is an Austrian girl who speaks

very little English. John and Yoko followed her back to her hotel room, entered it using a key they had somehow managed to obtain, and filmed her while she frantically telephoned for help! The picture was later cut to about 40 minutes running time.

In October 1969 a number of short films by John and Yoko received a four-hour long screening at the Institute of Contemporary Arts in London. Some 400 persons, mostly members of London's New Cinema Club, attended the preview showing. They paid about $2.50 each for the privilege of seeing the movies.

The pictures screened on that occasion included *Rape—Part II, Two Virgins, Honeymoon* and *Self-Portrait*. Of these the half-hour *Self-Portrait* is probably the most controversial since it displays a frontally nude John Lennon. The sounds accompanying this film footage are of planes, birds and cars rushing by. The program notes explained that, "The result is translucent and hypnotic and mystifying. The combination of slow motion and outdoor sound is perfectly balanced, thus neutralizing the awareness of its technology."

A compilation of six films by John and Yoko was released commercially in April 1972. The 99 minute program included *Rape—Part II* (40 minutes) *Fly* (25 minutes), *Erection* (19 minutes), *The Ballad of John and Yoko* (3 minutes), *Cold Turkey* (6 minutes) and *Apotheosis* (6 minutes).

Just as *Rape—Part II* had nothing to do with conventional rape and *Self-Portrait* was anything but a conventional self-portrait of the artist, *Erection* is an equally misleading title. What is deals with is the construction of a London hotel over an 18-month period. Still photographer Iain MacMillan took pictures of the building as it took shape over this time span, and these photographs were put on film so as to give the effect of the building blooming like a flower right before our eyes.

Fly stars a fly and a naked girl. The insect explores the

nude girl's body for most of the picture, and is joined by some other flies at the end. Both *Fly* and *Apotheosis* were screened in May 1971 at the Cannes Film Festival's French Film Director Fortnight. Reportedly, *Fly* was the better received of the two shorts.

The Ballad of John and Yoko was shown in Frankfurt in August 1969 in combination with another short called *Number 5*, which ran 52 minutes together and was said to show "three minutes in the life of John and Yoko." A *Variety* report (8/20/69) said that "teenage fans responded with jeers and screams" to the screening. Apparently, *Ballad* was trimmed considerably for its commercial release in the compilation of short films.

Cold Turkey is another short film documentary about the public lives of John and Yoko. *Apotheosis* presents images of a snow-covered village as seen from a camera ascending through the clouds attached to a balloon.

In reviewing the compilation of films by John and Yoko *Boxoffice* (6/5/72) said, "it's a foregone conclusion that the hysterics attendant to the first onslaught of The Beatles' motion pictures in the U.S. market a decade ago has well subsided as far as commercial play-off of this sextet is concerned. But to specialized situations and, particularly, to theatres catering to the so-called young adult college crowd, the (compilation) should prove engrossing entertainment."

The same pictures were screened in Los Angeles in February 1972 along with a seventh short, *Give Peace A Chance*. Kevin Thomas reviewed them in the *Los Angles Times* (2/12/72), commenting that they "might be twice as good if they were only half as long." He pointed out that "the Lennons clearly take themselves seriously. As it turns out they are worth taking seriously — to a degree."

He described *Give Peace A Chance* (3 minutes) as "a straight-forward documentary on one of their (John and Yoko's) highly publicized Bed-Ins for Peace."

Mr. Thomas wrote that, "It's tempting to dismiss *The*

Films of John and Yoko Lennon...as the biggest put-on since Andy Warhol turned a camera on a sleeping man (or the Empire State Building) and let it run for eight hours."

The difference, he explained, was that Warhol "Had the honesty to say the great thing about his early efforts was that you didn't have to bother seeing them," whereas John and Yoko "clearly take themselves seriously."

(12) *LET IT BE* — A United Artists release. An Apple production. Produced by Neil Aspinall. Directed by Michael Lindsay-Hogg. Photography: Tony Richmond, Les Parrott and Paul Bond. Edited by Tony Lenny and Graham Gilding. Sound: Peter Sutton, Roy Mingaye and Ken Reynolds. Filmed in 16mm and blown up to 35mm for commerical distribution. Filmed in Technicolor. MPAA rating: G. Running time: 80 minutes.

Cast: John Lennon, Paul McCartney, George Harrison, Ringo Starr, Billy Preston and Yoko Ono.

Reviews: The release of *Let It Be* followed the news that The Beatles were breaking up. Many reviewers made mention of that information in their pieces about the film. *Daily Viariety's Rick.* noted (5/13/70) that although the picture "is a relatively innocuous, unimaginative piece of film," it is fascinating because it is "probably the last public appearance of Paul McCartney, John Lennon, George Harrison and Ringo Starr as a group. With all the gossip and speculation attending the split, reading between the spoken lines of the film beccomes a game in itself."

He went on to predict — and correctly so, as things have turned out to date — that "It is McCartney, the baby-faced idol of the 1960s, now bearded, dark and striking-looking, who will probably emerge strongest as a major individual talent of the 1970s as a composer and singer."

Commenting on the film's technical qualities, he called

the outdoor concert photography "muddy, and the long-lens close-ups, shot from surrounding roofs, are off-focus." The concert, of course is the famous one done by The Beatles on the roof of Apple's Savile Row office building. It tied up traffic in the London streets below for many blocks as people gathered together to see what was happening on the roof of Apple!

In *The Hollywood Reporter* (5/13/70) it was noted that, "The film is blown up from 16mm, sometimes a bit quavering, sometimes annoyingly halated, out of focus, but acceptable under the circumstances. Certain segments have been seen on the Ed Sullivan Show in lieu of live appearance. The same and other clips were distributed to national and local rock shows. The amortization of an originally low budget is the key to the profits the picture will earn."

The value of the film was said to be that "it preserves a moment in time and a view of the working manner — sober and professional for the most part — of the most important entertainment personalities of the past decade, whose growth has almost always exceeded our own, a growth which made parting inevitable."

The Los Angeles *Times'* Charles Champlin made the point (5/20/70) that, "Whether they have split for good or whether (probably) they haven't, the Beatles continue to be the single most extraordinary pop music phenomenon of the post-swing era, with an interest and an influence which has gone far beyond music." He called *Let It Be* "every bit as interesting as the now-classic feature films they did with Richard Lester."

He also found that "it makes for the warmest and most engaging hour and a half of film I've seen in weeks, maybe longer. It is also an immensely interesting glimpse at these four pleasant and talented young men who constitute so large a hunk of social history."

A very different view was taken by Sheilah Graham in the Hollywood *Citizen-News* (5/30/70). She wrote that

Let It Be "should have been aborted in the cutting room." In her view, "it is a good thing that the Beatles are now going their separate ways."

Penelope Gilliatt reviewed *Let It Be* for *The New Yorker*, calling it "a very bad film and a touching one — about change, about the breaking apart of this reassuring, geometrically perfect, once apparently ageless family of siblings."

She observed that The Beatles had provided the public with "jaunty survivalism without threats, which is a missing combination in America at the moment; heresay, which we need, and and no chaos." And she concluded that, "Now they are splitting up, and finding work difficult, and while we benefit from the risks they took, they sing songs filled with variants of self-addressed lines about 'Get back to where you once belonged'."

Esquire (August 1970) called the film "a sad and fascinating Apple home movie." It went on to charge that it "is a sloppy piece of intramural ripoff, with a special bummer of a sound track. But its crudity only makes us strain the harder to catch the aside, the gesture that will reveal them to us, lay bare the education of their fabulous odyssey together."

The magazine concluded that "They've regularly surpassed and redefined our expectations for nearly a decade. They've brought untellable happiness into our happiness-forsaken world. Now, in what looks like a collective bad head, they're busting up, with four individual lives still ahead of them. Fine your stars, please, Beatles."

In the Motion Picture *Herald* (6/17/70) Ron Pennington wrote that, "The spontaneity and crazy antics that were so much a part of their early films and appearances are now sadly missing. As the Beatles' music has steadily grown and progressed during the past decade, so have the Beatles themselves. They are no longer the close-knit group that used to seem to be having so much fun working together."

He also wrote that, "Whether or not George Harrison, John Lennon, Paul McCartney and Ringo Starr will ever work together as a group again remains to be seen. If they do not, it will be a sad loss to the music scene, although, hopefully, each will go on to make his own individual contribution. If they do get back together, it will be an answer to prayers of countless fans throughout the world. Let it be."

Addressing himself to the same point in the Los Angeles *Herald-Examiner* (5/22/70) Richard Cuskelly declared, "If it is indeed true that the Beatles will never perform again, then the music world has lost its most influential and creative group and the movie world has lost the only modern equivalent of the Marx Brothers. But is it really such a tragedy? Where yesterday we had one super-star group, today we have four superstars, each with his unique style and appeal."

He labeled the picture "the sprightliest, the liveliest and the most engaging funeral march ever composed."

Alexander Walker of the *Evening Standard* in London panned the movie, saying that "Fame has sated the Beatles to the point where they obviously can't care less."

To Felix Barker of the London *Evening News*, the movie's songs "ought to satisfy their fans. To the less committed, this may look more like the last whimper of a dying civilization."

What was it like filming *Let It Be*? Director Michael Lindsay-Hogg talked about it once, saying that The Beatles have "a strange sort of democracy. There is no majority. If one of them doesn't want to do something then there is no point in going ahead because the abstainer won't turn up." He apparently had wanted to get The Beatles To Africa to do a live concert, "but eventually I managed to persuade them up two flights of stars onto the Apple roff."

(13) *200 MOTELS* — A United Artists release.

Produced by Jerry Good and Herb Cohen. Written and directed by Frank Zappa and Tony Palmer. Photography: Tony Palmer. Film editor: Rich Harrison. Music by Frank Zappa. Production design: Cal Schenkel. Art direction: Leo Austin. Sound: Peter Hubbard and Robert Auger, Todd-AO. Assistant director: David Alexander. Animation director. Chuck Swenson. Filmed in Technicolor. MPAA rating: Running time: 98 minutes.

Cast: Frank Zappa, Theodore Bikel, Ringo Starr, Keith Moon, Jimmy Carl Black, Martin Licket, Janet Ferguson, Lucy Offerall, Don Preston, Motorhead Sherwood, Dick Barber, Pamela Miller, Mark Volman and Howard Kaylan

Reviews: *Daily Variety's* review (10/29/71) by *Murf.* made only passing mention of Ringo, saying that "Starr's okay cameo has him dressed up like Zappa." He called *200 Motels* "the zaniest piece of filmusical fantasy-comedy since *The Beatles' A Hard Day's Night* some seven years ago." He also pointed out that the picture "is the first in theatrical release to have been shot in the color vidtape-to-film process of Technicolor's Vidtronics subsid."

In *The Hollywood Reporter* Rochelle Reed (10/28/71) wrote that, "As participants, Ringo Starr, Theodore Bikel, the Mothers of Invention, and the Royal Philharmonic Orchestra might as well have been cardboard cutouts — something Zappa obviously intended, because he often used inflated dummies to double for the characters anyway."

She also quoted Ringo's statement at the beginning of the film to the effect that "Touring can make you crazy, and that's what *200 Motels* is all about."

Donald J. Mayerson reviewed the picture for *Cue* Magazine (11/20/71), noting that Frank Zappa "not only attempts unsuccessfully to imitate the freewheeling style of the Beatles' films, but also uses Ringo Starr as his comic stand-in."

(14) *RAGA* — An Apple Films release. Produced and directed by Howard Worth. Screenplay by Nancy Bacal. Executive producer: Gary Haber. Associate producer: Nancy Bacal. Photograph: Jimmy Allen. Film editor: Merle Worth. Sound: Chris Newman. Additional music: Colin Walcott. Filmed in Eastmancolor. Running time: 96 minutes.

Cast: Ravi Shankar, Alla Rakha, Yehudi Menuhin, Colin Walcott, George Harrison and Lakshmi Shankar.

Reviews: Although George Harrison was the moving force behind *Raga* — originally titled *Messenger Out of the East* — he did not play a major role in the film, itself. According to *Daily Variety's Gold.* (11/19/71) "Beatle George Harrison is seen briefly taking a sitar lesson."

Boxoffice magazine (11/22/71) also noted George's appearance in the picture, saying that "Old friend Yehudi Menuhin, one of the great violinists, joins Shankar for an informal session while youthful George Harrison comes to the master to learn."

In reporting on a press conference held by George Harrison and Ravi Shankar in Los Angeles in June 1968 to announce production of the film, *The Hollywood Reporter* (6/14/68) said that the picture will probe the culture and traditions of Indian music, art, philosophy, religion and life, centered around Shankar's own life and experiences."

(15) *BLINDMAN* — A Twentieth Century-Fox release. An ABKCO Film production. Produced by Tony Anthony and Saul Swimmer. Directed by Ferdinando Baldi. Executive producer: Roberto Infascelli. Screenplay by Tony Anthony, Piero Anchisi and Vincenzo Cerami. Based on an original story by Tony Anthony. Photography: Riccardo Pallotini. Film editor: Roberto Perpignani. Music: Stelvio Cipriani. Art direction: Gastone Carsetti. MPAA rating: R. Filmed in Technicolor. Running time: 105 minutes.

Cast: Tony Anthony, Ringo Starr, Agneta Eckemyr, Lloyd Batista, Magda Konopka and Raf Baldassarie.

Reviews: In *Daily Variety* (4/19/72) *Vine.* observed that "aided by a seeing-eye horse, and Ringo Starr, as one of the Mexican villains, also topbilled, pic may play off well as an action programmer." His only other mention of Ringo said he "is generally bland" in a "comparatively small role."

The Hollywood Reporter's Arthur Knight (4/10/72) wrote that, "As to Ringo Starr, the villain's equally villainous brother, he is successfully disguised behind a heavy beard, which seems the better part of valor."

(16) *THE CONCERT FOR BANGLA DESH* — A Twentieth Century-Fox release. Produced by George Harrison and Allen B. Klein. Directed by Saul Swimmer. Photography: Saul Negrin, Richard Brooks, Fred Hoffman and Tohru Nakamura. Film editor: Howard Lester. Music recording produced by George Harrison and Phil Spector. MPAA Rating: G. Running time: 99 minutes.

Cast: Eric Clapton, Bob Dylan, George Harrison, Billy Preston, Leon Russell, Ravi Shankar, Ringo Starr, Klaus Voorman, Badfinger, Jesse Davis, Jim Horn, Jim Keltner, Claudio Linnear and Carl Radle.

Reviews: The motion picture of the Madison Square Garden (New York City) *Concert For Bangla Desh* generally received enthusiastic reviews. *Time* magazine's critic, J.C., commented (4/17/72) that, "The musicians (Harrison, Leon Russell, Eric Clapton, Bob Dyland among them) were loose and enthusiastic, the audience wildly receptive. Together they generated the reciprocal excitement of a revival meeting."

In *Variety's* review (3/27/72) it was pointed out that, "In the case of ex-Beatle Harrison, audiences see for the first time some studio recorded material. Ringo Starr was reunited with Harrison and Bob Dylan emerged from seclusion."

Rober Hilburn, pop music critic for the Los Angeles *Times*, noted (3/27/72) that, "Though rock is often viewed as a hedonistic, thoughtless, exploitive musical form, there was a clear sense of purpose and artistry in mind last August when George Harrison and Ravi Shankar organized the now famous Madison Square Garden concert."

In his view, "despite slowness of the early scenes, you begin to appreciate the lack of razzle dazzle, the absence of the tiresome backstage scenes and the endless audience footage that so often mar rock music films."

The picture, originally filmed in 16mm by six cameras, was blown up to 70mm size for its commerical distribution.

Writing in *Films and Filming* (October 1972) Alex Stuart stated that, "As concert movies go, Bangla Desh is straight — extremely straight. There are no split-screen freak outs, no mind-blowing colour solarisations, no puberescent *Top Of The Pops-ish* camera tilts, a few triple dissolves maybe, but mainly it's just plain, unpretentious, unobtrusive shooting."

He went on to say that "it relies almost totally upon the musicians' performances for effect, and works very well. It is not Swimmer's self-indulgent turn on; neither is it an attempt to recreate on celluloid the original experience. It is merely an impression of the performances — the music — of the concert."

As for George's music, the critic said, "it becomes clear that while his music is fine and performs well, he lacks that certain spellbinding magic. At times he seems even to have to fight to make himself heard. However, I still enjoy his songs immensely."

In *The Hollywood Reporter* (3/27/72) Craig Fisher applauded the picture for not being "gussied up with optical effects." He wrote that, "the obvious fact is that watching a film of an event is not the same as watching the actual event, and the further fact is that most of these men are not, if they ever were, especially exciting performers. In person, they don't have to be, and perhaps I should make clear that, had I been at Madison Square Garden, I would probably have been on my feet along with everyone else. But they are not good camera subjects, and so, as if to compensate for this, Swimmer has to keep relying on huge, 70mm close-ups of them. The effect is that the screen is about to swallow them up."

(17) *BORN TO BOOGIE* — An Anglo-EMI presentation. An Apple Films production. Produced and directed by Ringo Starr. Photography: Nik Knowland, Richard Starkey, (Ringo Starr, of course), Mike Dodds, Mike Davis, Jeremy Stavenhagen and Richard Stanley. Track sound recording. Tony Victoni. Sound: Tony Jackson. Film editor: Graham Gilding. Filmed in Technicolor. Running time: 67 minutes.

Cast: Marc Bolan, lead singer, and members of British rock group T. Rex.

Reviews: Born to Boogie was a relatively minor picture about a concert by the British rock group T. Rex. According to *Daily Variety* (12/15/72) it was "scarcely and auspicious debut for Apple Films and former Beatle Ringo Starr (who also appears) as producer-director." The paper also said that, "Starr and his cohorts seemingly made no effort to perceive a 'happening' but only to record it, and not too imaginatively at that."

(18) *IMAGINE* — A Joko Films Production. Produced, directed and edited by John Lennon and Yoko Ono. Photography: John Lennon, Yoko Ono and Jonas Mekas. Music by John Lennon and Yoko Ono. Filmed in color. Running time: 70 minutes.

Cast: John Lennon, Yoko Ono, Fred Astaire, Jack Palance, Dick Cavett, George Harrison and Andy Warhol.

Reviews: Boxoffice magazine (1/22/73) observed that John and Yoko's staunchest fans may be expected to support" their film *Imagine,* but "Others may find it

187

vaguely amusing or bewildering or both."

The trade magazine added that, "Lennon's musical genius and outrageous sense of humor, evident since his early Beatle days, have not diminished but *Imagine* doesn't offer enough of either."

Playboy magazine reviewed the picture (May 1973), advising John that "maybe you and Yoko should think twice — or once, at any rate — before you start another movie."

(19) *THAT'LL BE THE DAY* — A Nat Cohen presentation. An Anglo-EMI Film-Goodtimes Enterprises production. Produced by David PUttnam and Sanford Lieberson. Directed by Claude Whatham. Screenplay by Ray Connolly. Based on an original story by Ray Connolly. Photography: Peter Suschitzky. Film editor: Michael Bradsell. Executive producer: Roy Baird. Music supervision: Neil Aspinall and Keith Moon. Filmed in Technicolor. Running time: 90 minutes.

Cast: David Essex, Ringo Starr, Rosemary Leach, James Booth, Billy Fury, Keith Moon, Rosalind Ayres, Robert Lindsay, Beth Morris, James Ottaway, Verna Harvey, Erin Geraghty and Deborah Watling.

Reviews: Ringo received generally good critical notices for his performance in *That'll Be The Day*. In *Variety* (11/19/73) Hawk remarked that "Ringo Starr is excellent (and his name can't hurt on the marquee)."

Alan R. Howard of *The Hollywood Reporter* wrote that, "Ringo Starr, who appears in bout 30 minutes of the film, is wonderfully well used, totally appealing and touchingly comic."

Charles Champlin reviewed the film for the Los Angeles *Times* (10/30/74), calling the performances by David Essex and Ringo "so assured and easy that they hardly seem like performances." He added that, "Ringo, a marvelously good and sympathetic actor, lets us understand a lot about the born survivor (his character in the film)."

Time magazine's review, signed J.C., agreed (12/16/74) that Ringo had done well, saying that his character was "played with wit and affection by none other than Ringo Starr."

(20) *LIVE AND LET DIE* — A United Artists release. Produced by Albert R. Broccoli and Harry Saltzman. Directed by Guy Hamilton. Screenplay by Tom mankiewicz. Based on the novel by Ian Fleming. Music by George Martin. Theme by Monty Norman. Title song by Paul and Linda McCartney. Film editors: Bert Bates, Raymond Pulton and John Shirley. Art directors: Syd Cain and Stephen Hendrickson. Sound: John Mitchell and Ken Barker. Assistant diretors: Derek Cracknell and Alan Hopkins. Photography: Ted Moore. Second unit photography: John Harris. Filmed in Color by DeLuxe. MPAA rating: P.G. Running time 121 minutes.

Cast: Roger Moore, Yaphet Kotto, Jane Seymour, Clifton James, Julius W. Harris, Geoffrey Holder, David Hedison, Gloria Hendry, Bernard Lee and Lois Maxwell.

Reviews: In his *Variety* (6/27/73) review *Murf.* noted that the "Emphasis in music billing is on Paul and Linda (Eastman) McCartney's title song, performed by McCartney and Wings; it is a serviceable melody, lacking the guts of previous Bond pix themes, but then in harmony with the current overall concept."

Paul and Linda McCartney's song, *Live And Let Die*, became one of the top records of 1973, bringing the movie a tremendous amount of publicity every time the song was played on the radio.

(21) *SON OF DRACULA* — A Cinemation Industries release. An Apple Films production. Produced by Ringo Starr. Directed by Freddie Francis. Screenplay by Jay Fairbank. Art director: Andrew Sanders. Photography: Norman Warwick. Music: Paul Buckmaster. Consultant editor: Derek York. Sound: Tony Jackson. Filmed in color. MPAA rating: PG. Running time: 90 minutes.

Cast: Harry Nelson, Ringo Starr, Freddie Jones,

Rosanna Lee, Dennis Price, Skip Martin and Dan Meaden.

Reviews: John H. Door reviewed the film for *The Hollywood Reporter* (12/2/74), deciding that "Ringo's production probably lacks the flash to grab a major audience, but it is an affectionate, worldly-wise attempt at something rather ambitious, its casualness finally working against its coherence."

He also wrote that "Ringo's flat, matter of fact underplaying purposefully kills the melodrama in civilized conversations about the eternal powers of the universe." Overall, he thought the film — Ringo's first production for Apple Films — was "a surprisingly serious, even intellectual, adaptation of horror film mythologies into an existential magic show presided over by Ringo himself as Merlin the Magician."

Talking about his work as a producer, Ringo once told an interviewer, "In the last two years I produced two movies and directed one, so that it was movie city for me. Out of it all, I think acting is the most comfortable deal. Directing I love to do. But producing will drive you insane. Producers are worth their weight in gold for getting all those things together because it ain't easy."

(22) *LITTLE MALCOLM AND HIS STRUGGLE AGAINST THE EUNUCHS* — A Multicetera release. An Apple Films and George Harrison presentation. Executive producer: George Harrison. Produced by Gavrik Losey. Directed by Stuart Cooper. Screenplay by Derek Woodward. Based on the play of the same name by David Halliwell. Photography: John Alcott. Film editor: Ray Lovejoy. Music: Stanley Myers. Filmed in Panavision and color. Running time: 112 minutes.

Cast: John Hurt, John McEnery, Raymond Platt, Rosalind Ayres and David Warner.

Reviews: Little Malcolm was reviewed in *Daily Variety* (7/11/74) by *Hawk.*, who saw it screened at the Berlin Film Festival. He called it "a frequently hilarious, generally thought-provoking and sobering, beautifully acted but a trifle overlong and repetitious film of uncertain destination, being a bit too special for general audiences and—in some passages — too rough for primetime vidspectators."

The film went on to capture the Silver Bear Award in Berlin. In August 1974 it was honored with a Gold Medal at the Atlanta Film Festival. It therefore, became a major achievement for George Harrison, its Executive Producer.

The film was the subject of a critique in *Films and Filming* (February 1975) by Gordon Gow. He called it "one of those rarities, an actor's film." In his view, "*Little Malcolm* is an essay on impotence; not only the sexual sort — although that, too — but the cronic inability to function, the malaise of the spirit which vents its frustrations in vicious fantasy or overt violence. In this case, both."

Based on a play of the same name performed in London in 1966, the movie centers on an art student, Malcolm Scrawdyke, who has been expelled from his school for being a bad influence. He vows to gain revenge by tricking the school's headmaster into destroying a valuable painting stolen from a gallery.

The 1976 edition of the *International Film Guide* stated that the picture "about the sexual and artistic frustration often to be found lurking behind the bombast of the student revolutionary, has no greater admirer than former Beatle George Harrison, who entirely financed this film version."

(23) *LISZTOMANIA* — A Warner Bros. release. Produced by Roy Baird. Co-produced by David Puttnam. Directed by Kenn Russell. Executive Producer: Sanford Lieberson. Screenplay by Ken Russell. Photograph: Peter Suschitzky. Musical arranger: Rick Wakeman. Production manager: Peter Price. Art director: Philip Harrison. Film editor: Stuart

Baird. Costume designer: Shirley Russell. Filmed in Panavision and Eastmancolor. MPAA rating: R. Running time: 105 minutes.

Cast: Roger Daltrey, Sara Kestelman, Paul Nicholas, Fiona Lewis, Veronica Quilligan, Nell Campbell, Andrew Reilly, Ringo Starr, John Justin, Anulka Dziubinska, Imogen Claire, Peter Brayham and David English.

Reviews: Lisztomania was reviewed in *The Hollywood Reporter* by Todd McCarthy, who observed that "Ringo Starr is fittingly loony as a Pope bedecked in robes featuring photographs of Judy Garland, Mickey Rooney and other Hollywood icons."

As for the film, itself, he wrote, "Ken Russell's latest binge of mad invention has produced *Lisztomania,* a film as stupid as it is inspired, as simple-minded as it is stunning. Russell's visual creativity has never been more outrageously potent than here, but it's almost as if the high-voltage rock of *Tommy* has frazzled th director's mind and caused him to lose his taste in music. Russell's fertile imagination seems to work in inverse ratio to his intelligence level."

(24) *I WANT TO HOLD YOUR HAND* — A Universal Studios release. Executive Producer: Steven Spielberg. Produced by Tamara Asseysev and Alex Rose. Directed by Robert Zemeckis. Screenplay by Robert Zemeckis and Bob Gale. Filmed for release in April 1978.

Cast: Susan Newman, Nancy Allen, Bobby DiCicco, Marc McClure, Theresa Saldana and Wendie Jo Sperber.

Background: Originally entitled *Beatles 4 Ever*, this nostalgic look at the 1960s focuses on the lives of a group of teenagers from Maplewood, N.J. whose lives are affected by the arrival of The Beatles in the U.S. The action takes place during a period of about 36 hours surrounding *The Beatles'* first appearance on *The Ed*

Sullivan Show on February 9, 1964. Carrie Fisher (*Star Wars*) was originally supposed to have starred in the film, but had to drop out for what the studio called "scheduling difficulties" and was replaced by Susan Newman. A cameo role in the film is played by former New York disc jockey Murray Kaufman, who as *Murry The K* became a close friend of *The Beatles* and was known, for a time, as The Fifth Beatle.

(25) *SGT. PEPPER'S LONELY HEARTS CLUB BAND* — A Universal Studios release in the United States and Canada. Produced by Robert Stigwood. Foreign distribution rights controlled by Robert Stigwood at press time. Directed by Michael Schultz. Screenplay by Henry Edwards. Filmed for release in December 1978.

Cast: Peter Frampton, The Bee Gees, George Burns, Donald Pleasence, Steve Martin, Alice Cooper, Aerosmith, Billy Preston and Earth, Wind and Fire. The grand finale features a star-studded chorus reportedly composed of: Peter Allen, Stephen Bishop, Keith Carradine, Carol Channing, Dr. John Donovan, Jose Feliciano, Johnny Rivers, Frankie Valli, Curtis Mayfield, Bruce Johnston, Nils Lofgren, Helen Reddy, Minnie Riperton, Chita Rivera, Seals & Crofts, Tina Turner, Gwen Verdon, Bobby Womack, Wolfman Jack and more!

Background: Robert Stigwood's production of *Sgt. Pepper's Lonely Hearts Club Band* is an elaborate $12 million salute to The Beatles. Like two of Mr. Stigwood's previous pictures, *Jesus Christ Superstar* and *Tommy*, the film of *Sgt. Pepper* will have no dialogue. It will be an all-singing movie. Its music will be drawn principally from The Beatles' albums *Sgt. Pepper* and *Abbey Road*, but other Beatles' songs will be used too.

There had been some speculation when plans were announced to film the picture's grand finale production number that The Beatles, themselves, might choose to make their reunion right there on the rented soundstage at the MGM Studios in Culver City, Calif. in December 1977. Of course, the reunion never took place. There was plenty of top stars (see *Cast* list above), but no real life Beatles.

Sgt. Pepper was presented as a Broadway musical, directed by Tom O'Horgan, in 1975. It ran for 66 performances and then disappeared. Mr. Stigwood once explained to a reporter that, "The original plan was to mount it on Broadway and then take it around to arenas around the country...The first time I saw the show, though, I was amazed to hear the audience singing the songs. I decided that the same thing would happen if it were done as a movie. I had the option of reworking the stage show, but I decided to close it down and rethink the whole project as a film."

To write his screenplay Mr. Stigwood hired rock music journalist Henry Edwards. He announced Chris Bearde to direct the project, but later gave the assignment to Michael Schult. Among Mr. Schultz's credits are the pictures *Cooley High, Car Wash* and *Which Way Is Up?*

As this book is written, there's no telling how successful the movie version of *Sgt. Pepper* will be. It certainly sounds like it should be a smash, but that doesn't guarantee anything, of course. Mr. Stigwood has gone on record as predicting that it will be even more successful than his considerable hit *Tommy* was. He was quoted by an interviewer as saying, "The music is less strident, more melodic. Although *Tommy* was an enormous box-office hit, the appeal of *Sg. Pepper* should be wider. We'll get the very young and the grandparents that you wouldn't get in to see *Tommy*."

XII

ALBUMANIA

The statistics The Beatles created in the music world are staggering. Consider these figures on their performance on platters:

*Twenty Number One records.
*More than sixty hit songs.
*More than thirty in the Top 10 portion of music charts.
*More than 85 million Beatles albums sold.
*A staggering 120 million singles records.

In addition to the enormous quantity, of course, there has also been enormous quality. To appreciate the extent of material available on records by The Beatles it is necessary to consider a directory such as the one that follows.

In this chapter The Beatles' albums and singles are listed in the order in which they were released in the United States. In many cases, of course, the release dates for the same albums and singles were different in the United Kingdom.

Also contained in this directory is information regarding the record company identification numbers for the albums or singles, the cuts included in each album, the flip side of each single, and the first initial of the lead singer on each song (e.g., J-John Lennon).

Virtually all of The Beatles' material has been released in the United States by Capital Records, the American arm of the English company EMI/Parlophone, which originally signed The Beatles in 1962.

Starting with The Beatles' album called simply *The Beatles*, but known to fans as *The White Album*

(November 1968 the group's discs were released on their own Apple Records label and distributed in the U.S. by Capitol.

Because in the early days of The Beatles Capitol Records was not eager to release their material in the U.S., some early Beatle singles were put out in America on the Swan Records and VJ Records labels. Swan issued one single from The Beatles in August 1963, consisting of *She Loves You* on the "A" or principal side, and *I'll Get You* on the "B" or flip side. In May 1964 Swan put out a second Beatle single called *Sie Liebt Dich.*

The VJ singles, which were released in late 1963 and early 1964, were: *Please, Please Me/Ask Me Why; From Me To You/Thank You Girl; Do You Want To Know A Secret/Twist And Shout;* and *Love Me Do/P.S. I Love You.*

VJ later released two albums of Beatle material in 1964, after Capitol was the group's official American distributor. The first of the VJ albums was called *Introducing the Beatles: Songs, Pictures and Stories of the Fabulous Beatles.* The second LP was entitled *Jolly What!—The Beatles and Frank Ifield On Stage.*

The soundtrack to The Beatles' first movie, *A Hard Day's Night,* was released on the United Artists Records label in June 1964. UA was also the distributor of the film, itself.

A particularly fascinating album of vintage material by The Beatles is available on Polydor Records (#24-4504) under the title *The Beatles Featuring Tony Sheridan—In The Beginning (Circa 1960).* It contains 12 cuts recorded by the early Beatles, who were working in Hamburg, Germany, at the time as a back-up band for singer Tony Sheridan.

The LP cuts on Side One are: *Ain't She Sweet,* The Beatles, John Lennon vocal; *Cry For A Shadow,* The Beatles; *Let's Dance,* Tony Sheridan and The Beat Brothers; *My Bonnie,* The Beatles with Tony Sheridan vocal; *Take Out Some Insurance On Me, Baby,* The Beatles with Tony Sheridan vocal; *What'd I Say,* Tony Sheridan and The Beat Brothers.

On Side Two of the Polydor LP are these cuts: *Sweet Georgia Brown,* The Beatles with Tony Sheridan vocal; *The Saints,* The Beatles with Tony Sheridan vocal; *Ruby Baby,* Tony Sheridan and The Beat Brothers; *Why,* The Beatles with Tony Sheridan; *Nobody's Child,* The Beatles with Tony Sheridan vocal; *and Ya-Ya,* Tony Sheridan and The Beat Brothers.

As most Beatle fans already know, The Beatles' drummer in 1960 was Pete Best. He was replaced by Ringo Starr just before The Beatles cut their first British hit record, *Love Me Do,* on September 11, 1962.

Best is pictured along with John, Paul and George on the cover of the Polydor LP, which displays the front page of the newspaper *Mersey Beat* for January 4-18, 1962. The headline declares *BEATLES TOP POLL!*

A photograph of the group by Albert Marrion takes up virtually the rest of the front page above the fold. Other photos of The Beatles from the early 1960s are included inside the album jacket, along with extensive liner notes by Tony Sheridan. It's truly a collector's item, although it was issued years after The Beatles came to fame.

The earliest Beatle albums distributed in Great Britain differ from their American counterparts in that there are more cuts on the English LPs. Fourteen selections are included in most of the English albums, while there are generally only twelve cuts on the LPs released in the United States.

The cuts dropped from the American albums tended, of course, to be lesser material such as cover versions by The Beatles of records already successfully released by other artists. American Beatle fans should not feel cheated, although they would undoubtedly prefer to have on file everything ever recorded by the group.

The first Beatles' album released in the U.S. by Capitol

Records was *MEET THE BEATLES* (ST-2047) on January 20, 1964. *Side One:* I Want To Hold Your Hand (J, P, G); I Saw Her Standing There (J, P); This Boy (J, P, G); It Won't Be Long (J); All I've Got To Do (P); All My Loving (P). *Side Two:* Don't Bother Me (G); Little Child (J, P); Till There Was You (P); Hold Me Tight (P); I Wanna Be Your Man (R); Not A Second Time (J).

Appropriately enough, the follow-up LP was called *THE BEATLES' SECOND ALBUM* (ST-2080). It was released by Capitol on April 10, 1964. *Side One:* Roll Over Beethoven (G0; Thank You Girl (J, P); You Really Got A Hold On Me (J, G); Devil In Her Heart (G); Money (J); You Can't Do That (J). *Side Two:* Long Tall Sally (P); I'll Call Your Name (J); Please, Mr. Postman (J, P, G); I'll Get You (J, P); She Loves You (J, P).

The third Beatles' album was the soundtrack to their first motion picture, *A HARD DAY'S NIGHT* (UAS-3366A), released by United Artists Records on June 26, 1964. *Side One:* A Hard Day's Night (J, P); Tell Me Why (J); I Cry Instead (J); I Should Have Known Better *(instrumental);* I'm Happy Just To Dance With You (G); And I Love Her *(instrumental); Side Two:* I Should Have Known Better (J); If I Fell (J, P); And I Love Her (P); Ringo's Theme—This Boy *(instrumental);* Can't Buy Me Love (P); A Hard Day's Night *(instrumental).*

The group's fourth album, *SOMETHING NEW* (ST-2108), was released on July 20, 1964. *Side One:* I'll Cry Instead (J, P); Things We Said Today (P); Any Time AT All (J); When I Get Home (J); Slow Down (J); Matchbox (R). *Side Two:* Tell Me Why (P, J); And I Love Her (P); I'm Happy Just To Dance With You (G); If I Fell (J, P); Komm, Gib Mir Deine Hand (J, P, G).

A documentary two-record LP called *THE BEATLES' STORY* (STBO-2222) was the group's fifth American album, released by Capitol on November 23, 1964. *Side One:* On Stage With The Beatles; How Beatlemania Began; Beatlemania In Action; Man Behind

The Beatles—Brian Epstein; John Lennon; Who's A Millionaire? *Side Two:* The Beatles Look At Life; "Victims" of Beatlemania; Beatle Medley; Ringo Starr; Liverpool And All The World. *Side Three:* Beatles Will Be Beatles; Man Behind The Music—George Martin; George Harrison. *Side Four:* A Hard Day's Night Their First Movie; Paul McCartney; Sneaky Haircuts And More About Paul.

The Beatles' sixth album, *BEATLES '65* (ST-2228), was released by Capitol on December 15, 1964. *Side One:* No Reply (J, P, G); I'm A Loser (J); Baby's In Black (J,P); Rock & Roll Music (J); I'll Follow The Sun (P); Mr. Moonlight (J). *Side Two:* Honey Don't (R); I'll Be Back (J); She's A Woman (P); I Feel Fine (J, P, G); Everybody's Trying To Be My Baby (G).

Album number seven was *THE EARLY BEATLES* (ST-2309), released on March 22, 1965 by Capitol. *Side One:* Love Me Do (J, P, G); Twist And Shout (J); Anna (J); Chains (J, P, G); Boys (R); Ask Me Why (J). *Side Two:* Please, Please Me (J, P, G); P.S. I Love You (P); Baby, It's You (J); A Taste Of Honey (P); Do You Want To Know A Secret (G).

The group's eighth American LP was called *BEATLES VI* (ST-2358), a somewhat misleading title since it didn't take into account the group's soundtrack on the UA label or its documentary album. It was released by Capitol on June 14, 1965. *Side One:* Kansas City (P); Eight Days A Week (J, P, G); You Like Me Too Much (G); Bad Boy (J); I Don't Want To Spoil The Party (J, P); Words Of Love (J, P). *Side Two:* What You're Doing (P); Yes, It Is (J, P, G, with a solo by J); Dizzy Miss Lizzie (J); Tell Me What You See (J, P); Every Little Thing (J, P).

HELP! (SMAS-2386), the soundtrack to The Beatles' second movie, was released by Capitol on August 13, 1965. It was the group's ninth major album in the U.S. *Side One:* Help! (J); The Night Before (P, J, G); You've

Got To Hide Your Love Away (J); I Need You (G, J, P); In The Tyrol *(instrumental). Side Two:* Another Girl (P, J, G); Ticket To Ride (J); Another Hard Day's Night *(instrumental);* The Bitter End/You Can't Do That *(instrumental);* You're Gonna Lose That Girl (J, G, P); The Chase *(instrumental).*

The Beatles' tenth American LP was *RUBBER SOUL* (ST-2442), released by Capitol on December 6, 1965. *Side One:* I've Just Seen A Face (P); Norwegian Wood (J); You Won't See Me (P); Think For Yourself (G); The Word (J, P, G); Michelle (P). *Side Two:* It's Only Love (J, P); Girl (J); I'm Looking Through You (P); In My Life (J, P); Wait (J, P); Run For Your Life (J).

YESTERDAY...AND TODAY (ST-2553), the group's eleventh album in America, was released by Capitol on June 20, 1966. *Side One:* Drive My Car (J, P); I'm Only Sleeping (J); Nowhere Man (J, P, G, R); Dr. Robert (J); Yesterday (P); Act Naturally (R). *Side Two:* And Your Bird Can Sing (J); If I Needed Someone (G); We Can Work It Out (J, P, G, R); What Goes On? (R); Day Tripper (J, P, G, R).

On August 8, 1966 Capitol released *REVOLVER* (ST-2576), considered by many people to be the first album in The Beatles' period of serious music. It was their twelfth American LP. *Side One:* Taxman (G); Eleanor Rigby (P); Love You Too (G); Here, There And Everywhere (P); Yellow Submarine (R); She Said She Said (J). *Side Two:* Good Day Sunshine (P); For No One (P); I Want To Tell You (G); Got To Get You Into My Life (P); Tomorrow Never Knows (J).

Album number thirteen was anything but unlucky! *SGT. PEPPER'S LONELY HEARTS CLUB BAND* (SMAS-2653), was released by Capitol on June 2, 1967. *Side One:* Sgt. Pepper's Lonely Hearts Club Band (P); A Little Help From My Friends (R); Lucy In The Sky With Diamonds (J); Getting Better (P); Fixing A Hole (P); She's Leaving Home (J, P); Being For The Benefit Of Mr.

Kite (J). *Side Two:* Within You Without You (G); When I'm Sixty-Four (P); Lovely Rita (P); Good Morning, Good Morning (J); Sgt. Pepper's Lonely Hearts Club Band *(reprise);* A Day In The Life (J, P).

MAGICAL MYSTERY TOUR (SMAL-2835), released by Capitol on November 27, 1967, was The Beatles' fourteenth American LP. *Side One:* Magical Mystery Tour (J, P, G, R); The Fool On The Hill (P); Flying *(instrumental);* Blue Jay Way (G); Your Mother Should Know (P); I Am The Walrus (J). *Side Two:* Hello, Goodbye (J, P, G, R); Strawberry Fields Forever (J); Penny Lane (P); Baby, You're A Rich Man (J, P); All You Need Is Love (J).

The group's fifteenth American album was *THE BEATLES* (SWBO-101), released by Capitol on November 25, 1968. It became known as *The White Album* because of its plain white packaging. This double album was the first album issued on the Apple Records label. *Side One:* Back In The U.S.S.R. (P); Dear Prudence (J); Glas Onion (J); Obladi Oblada (P); Wild Honey Pie (P); Bungalow Bill (J); While My Guitar Gently Weeps (G); Happiness Is A Warm Gun (J). *Side Two:* Martha My Dear (P); I'm So Tired (J); Blackbird (P); Piggies (G); Rocky Racoon (P); Don't Pass Me By (R); Why Don't We Do It In The Road (P); I Will (P); Julia (J). *Side Three:* Birthday (P); Yer Blues (J); Mother Nature's Son (P); Everybody's Got Something To Hide Except Me And My Monkey (J); Sexy Sadie (J); Helter Skelter (P); Long, Long, Long (G). *Side Four:* Revolution No. 1 (J); Honey Pie (P); Savoy Truffle (GP); Cry Baby Cry (J); Revolution No. 9 (J); Goodnight (R).

The Beatles' *YELLOW SUBMARINE* (SW-153), was their sixteenth LP in the U.S. On the Apple label, it was released by Capitol on January 13, 1969. *Side One:* Yellow Submarine (R); Only A Northern Song (G); All Together Now (P); Hey Bulldog (J); It's All Too Much (G); All You Need Is Love (J). *Side Two:* original film music composed and orchestrated by George Martin—Pepperland; Medley: Sea Of Time & Sea Of Holes; Sea of Monsters; March Of The Meanies; Pepperland Laid Waste; Yellow Submarine In Pepperland.

Beatles' album seventeen in American was *ABBEY ROAD* (SO-383), also on Apple and distributed by Capitol. It was released on October 1, 1969. *Side One:* Come Together (J); Something (G); Maxwell's Silver Hammer (P); Oh! Darling (P); Octopus's Garden (R); I Want You (She's So Heavy) (J). *Side Two:* Here Comes The Sun (P); Because (G); You Never Give Me Your Money (P); Sun King (G); Polythene Pam (J); Mean Mr. Mustard (J); She Came In Through The Bathroom Window (P); Golden Slumbers (P); Carry That Weight (J); The End (J, P, G, R); Her Majesty (P).

HEY JUDE (SW-385), the eighteenth American LP by the group, was on the Apple label Capitol released it on February 23, 1970. *Side One:* Can't Buy Me Love (P, J); I Should Have Known Better (J); Paperback Writer (P); Rain (J); Lady Madonna (P); Revolution (J). *Side Two:* Hey Jude (P); Old Brown Shoe (J); Don't Let Me Down (J); Ballad Of John & Yoko (J).

The last album by The Beatles, *LET IT BE* (ARS-34001), was the group's nineteenth LP distributed in America. It was on the Apple label, and was released by United Artists on May 15, 1970. *Side One:* Two Of Us (J, P); I Dig A Pony (J); Across The Universe (J); I Me Mine (G); Dig It (J); Let It Be (P); Maggie Mae (J). *Side Two:* I've Got A Feeling (P); One After 909 (J, P); The Long And Winding Road (P); For You Blue (G); Get Back (P).

In 1970 The Beatles broke up as a group, and issued no new albums as a group. On April 2, 1973 Capitol released two collections of the group's records—*THE BEATLES 1962-66* (SKBO-3403) and *THE BEATLES 1967-70* (SKBO-3404). These were collector's albums rather than

LPs built around a specific theme.

On June 11, 1976 Capitol launched the Beatles revival with the release of the album *ROCK 'N' ROLL MUSIC* (SKBO-11537). The LP features hard rock music by The Beatles, along with flashy modern-looking graphics. The album was packaged in a silver foil jacket with an artist's painting of The Beatles as they had looked in the early '60s. The inside of the double album spotlighted more items of the early- and pre-Beatle period—a vintage Chevrolet; a hamburger; a drive-in movie with Marilyn Monroe's face on the screen; a juke box; a soft drink in a glass similar to the old Coca Cola soda fountain glasses; and lots of records! The effort of all this was to evoke a long-gone era of musical history.

ROCK 'N' ROLL MUSIC included on *Side One:* Twist and Shout (from *The Early Beatles*, 1965); I Saw Her Standing There (from *Meet The Beatles*, 1964); You Can't Do That (from *The Beatles' Second Album*, 1964); I Wanna Be Your Man (from *Meet The Beatles*, 1964); I Call Your Name (from *The Beatles' Second Album*, 1964); Boys (from *The Early Beatles*, 1965); and Long Tall Sally (from *The Beatles' Second Album*, 1964).

Side Two consisted of: Rock & Roll Music (from *Beatles '65*, 1964); Slow Down (from *Something New*, 1964); Kansas City (from *Beatles VI*, 1965); Money (That's What I Want) (from *The Beatles' Second Album*, 1964); Bad Boy (from *Beatles VI*, 1965); Matchbox (from *Something New*, 1964); and Roll Over Beethoven (from *The Beatles' Second Album*, 1964).

Side Three spotlighted: Dizzy Miss Lizzie (from *Beatles VI*, 1965); Anytime At All (from *Something New*, 1964); Drive My Car (from *Yesterday...And Today*, 1966); Everybody's Trying To Be My Baby (from *Beatles '65* 1964); The Night Before (from *Help!*, 1965); I'm Down (released as a single in 1965); and Revolution (released as a single in 1968 and as part of the album *Hey Jude* in 1970).

Side Four focused on: Back In The U.S.S.R. (from *The Beatles,* 1968); Helter Skelter (from *The Beatles,* 1968); Taxman (from *Revolver,* 1966); Got To Get You Into My Life (from *Revolver,* 1966); Hey Bulldog (from *Yellow Submarine,* 1969); Birthday (from *The Beatles,* 1968); and Get Back (from *The Beatles/1967-70,* 1973).

The success that Capitol enjoyed with this repackaging of old Beatle material led to the release of another "new" Beatles album, *THE BEATLES AT THE HOLLYWOOD BOWL* (SMAS-11638), on May 4, 1977. The Beatles had performed at the Hollywood Bowl in Los Angeles during their American tours of 1964 and 1965. The concerts had been taped on the nights of August 23, 1964 and August 29, 1965. But the tapes had been of less than the best quality due to the nature of the recording situation—an *outdoor* concert before some 17,000 *screaming* fans. The *three track* recordings were of songs that The Beatles had previously released as perfect studio records. Hence, nothing ever was done with these live tapes.

Capitol, however, realized that these were the only live tapes of The Beatles performing (other than so-called bootleg or illegally recorded tapes). The company asked George Martin, who had produced The Beatles' records up until the *Let It Be* album, which was produced by Phil Spector, to listen to the Hollywood Bowl tapes and see if it would be possible to get them in shape for release now.

In his extensive liner notes on the LP George Martin explains how the old three-track recordings were transferred to top quality modern studio equipment for remixing, filtering, equalizing and editing. The result was a superb album which enriches any Beatle fan's collection.

Side One of *THE BEATLES AT THE HOLLYWOOD BOWL* included: Twist And Shout (8/30/65); She's A Woman (8/30/65); Dizzy Miss Lizzie (8/30/65); Ticket To Ride (8/30/65); Can't Buy Me Love

(8/30/65); Things We Said Today (8/23/64); and Roll Over Beethoven (8/23/64).

Side Two consisted of: Boys (8/23/64); A Hard Day's Night (8/30/65); Help! (8/30/65); All My Loving (8/23/64); She Loves You (8/23/64); and Long Tall Sally (8/23/64).

The packaging of the album featured copies of the original concert tickets on the front cover—J 17 38, a $4.00 reserved seat for the August 23, 1964 performance; and Box 1041, a $5.00 seat for the August 29, 1965 concert—and a variety of Beatles' memorabilia (buttons, pennants, books and a tray superimposed on a two-page black and white photo of the group performing at the Hollywood Bowl).

The most ambitious of Capitol's Beatles revival projects is the album *LOVE SONGS* (SKBL-11711), released on October 24, 1977. This double album is packaged in a simulated leather jacket, with a Richard Avedon black and white photograph of the group spread across the two inside pages. The same artwork is embossed in gold foil on the front cover. A large booklet containing the lyrics to all twenty-five songs featured on the album is included with the discs.

Side One contains: Yesterday; I'll Follow The Sun; I Need You; Girl; In My Life; Words Of Love, and Here, There And Everywhere.

Side Two includes: Something; And I Love Her; If I Fell; I'll Be Back; Tell Me What You See; and Yes, It Is.

Side Three features: Michelle; It's Only Love; You're Going To Lose That Girl; Every Little Thing; For No One; and She's Leaving Home.

Side Four concludes with: The Long And Winding Road; This Boy; Norwegian Wood; (This Bird Has Flown); You've Got To Hide Your Love Away; I Will; and P.S. I Love You.

The success of all three of the repackaged Beatles albums suggests that Capitol Records will probably release others in the future. Exactly what they will be is impossible to say at the moment, but it seems logical to guess that they will be built around theme lines the way *LOVE SONGS*, for instance, was.

Anyone who acquired every one of The Beatles' albums listed above would have a complete library of their LPs. Although they have all done albums since their split in 1970, there are no other albums in existence by The Beatles as a group.

To this collection of LPs can only be added a collection of single records by The Beatles. The list of singles released in the United Kingdom and in the United States varies somewhat in the early Beatle period.

Originally, Capitol Records was not anxious to distribute the group's songs in America, so they went to two much smaller labels, VJ and Swan. When it became apparent that The Beatles really were hitting the big time, Capitol changed its mind and grabbed them at the last minute.

Capitol's English parent, EMI/Parlophone had released The Beatles' records in the United Kingdom from the start.

In fairness to Capitol it should be pointed out that (a) the company's management today is different than it was in those days, and that today's Capitol is an astute and enthusiastic promoter of Beatle material; and (b) in the early 1960s no one had any idea just how big The Beatles could be in the U.S. The Capitol Records management at that time was not alone in failing to predict what was going to happen to John, Paul, George and Ringo.

After the 1963 and 1964 releases on VJ and Swan described earlier in this chapter, Capitol took over American distribution for The Beatles.

The first Beatle single to come out on the Capitol label was *I Want To Hold Your Hand/I Saw Her Standing There* (#5112), released on January 13, 1964. *I Want To Hold Your Hand* was played for the first time in

American on New York radio station WMCA on December 29, 1963 at 12:50 p.m. The disc had come out in England on November 29, 1963.

The next American single for The Beatles was *Can't Buy Me Love/You Can't Do That* (#5150), released on March 30, 1964. It had been issued in England on March 20, 1964.

On May 11, 1964 Capitol released an extended play single by The Beatles, *Roll Over Beethoven/All My Loving/This Boy/Please Mr. Postman* (EAP-2121). It has since been deleted from Capitol's catalogue.

The single that followed was *A Hard Day's Night/I Should Have Known Better* (#5222), released in the U.S. on July 13, 1964 and July 10, 1964 in England.

Next came *I'll Cry Instead/I'm Happy Just To Dance With You* (#5234), issued on July 20, 1964 in the U.S. Both songs were from the LP *Something New*. They were not released as singles in England.

The single that followed, *And I Love Her/If I Fell* (#5235), was also released in the U.S. on July 20, 1964. Those songs, too, were from *Something New*. They were not put out as a single in England.

Slow Down/Matchbox (#5255) was released in the U.S. on August 24, 1964. They, too, came from the album *Something New*, and had no release as singles in the United Kingdom.

The next major single from The Beatles was *I Feel Fine/She's A Woman* (#5327), released in American on August 24, 1964. Its release in England followed on November 27, 1964.

Another extended play single followed in the U.S. It consisted of *Honey Don't/I'm A Loser/Mr. Moonlight/Everybody's Trying To Be My Baby* (#5365). It was released on February 1, 1965, and has since been deleted from Capitol's catalogue.

Eight Days A Week/I Don't Want To Spoil The Party (#5371) came out in the U.S. on February 15, 1965. Both songs were from the album *Beatles VI*. They were not given single release in Great Britain.

Ticket To Ride/Yes It Is (#5407) had its American release on April 19, 1965, shortly after its appearance in England on April 9.

The next Beatles' single *Help!/I'm Down* (#5476), was released in American on July 19, 1965. It came out in England on July 23, 1965.

Yesterday/Act Naturally (#5498) was issued in the U.S. on September 13, 1965. Both cuts were from the album *Yesterday...And Today*. There was no release of this material as a single in the United Kingdom.

The Beatles' next American single was *We Can Work It Out/Day Tripper* (#5555), released on December 6, 1965. It was released in England on December 3, 1965, but with *Day Tripper* as the "A" side.

Nowhere Man/What Goes On (#5587) was issued in the U.S. on February 7, 1966. Both songs were from *Yesterday...And Today*. They were not released as an English single.

The group's next single, *Paperback Writer/Rain* (#5651), was released in the U.S. on May 23, 1966. It had its British release on June 10, 1966.

Yellow Submarine/Eleanor Rigby (#5715) appeared in the U.S. on August 5, 1966. It was released in England on August 8, 1966, but with *Eleanor Rigby* as the "A" side.

Next to appear was *Strawberry Fields Forever/Penny Lane* (#5810). Its American release was on February 13, 1967. It was issued in Great Britain on February 17, but with *Penny Lane* as the "A" side.

The single that followed was *Baby, You're A Rich Man/All You Need Is Love* (#5964). It was taken from The *Magical Mystery Tour LP*. Its American release was on July 24, 1967. There was no English release as a single.

Hello Goodbye/I Am The Walrus (#2056) was released in the U.S. on November 27, 1967. Its release in the United Kingdom had been on November 24, 1967.

The next single from The Beatles was *Lady Madonna/The Inner Light* (#2138), released in American on March 18, 1968. It was put out in England on March 15, 1968.

Hey Jude/Revolution (#2276), followed as a single. It was released in America on August 26, 1968 and in the United Kingdom on August 30, 1968.

It was followed by *Get Back/Don't Let Me Down* (#2490), issued on the Apple label in the U.S. on May 5, 1969 following its English release on April 15, 1969.

Next came *The Ballad Of John and Yoko/Old Brown Shoe* (#2531), released on the Apple label in America on June 16, 1969. It had been released in England on May 30, 1969.

Something/Come Together (#2654) appeared on the Apple label in the U.S. on October 13, 1969. It had its British release on October 31, 1969.

Then came *Let It Be/You Know My Name* (#2764), released on the Apple label in the U.S. on March 16, 1970. Its release the previous month in England marked the last Beatle single to come out there.

On May 25, 1970 Capitol released in the U.S. as a single *The Long And Winding Road/For You Blue* (#2832), both of which were on the Apple label and came from the *Let It Be* album.

Six years passed without any new Beatle singles. On May 31, 1976 Capitol released *Got To Get You Into My Life/Helter Skelter* (#4274) as an American single. *Got To Get You Into My Life* had been on the 1966 *Revolver* LP. *Helter Skelter* was one of the cuts on *The Beatles,* the double *White Album* of 1968. Neither had previously been issued in single form.

The last Beatles' single released by Capitol was *Ob-la-di, Ob-la-da* (#4347) on November 1, 1976. It too, had come from the *White Album,* and had never been released as a single before.

It remains to be seen if Capitol will issue "new" Beatles

singles as well as "new" Beatles LPs in the future. In view of the success of *Got To Get You Into My Life* as a single, it's altogether possible that Capitol might try its hand at another effort in the singles' market.

XIII
BEATLES SINGLE DISCOGRAPHY

The Beatles didn't just lay back and collect royalty checks after their breakup in 1970. John, Paul, George, and Ringo each went out on their own and turned out an impressive number of solo albums.

John's activity ceased after 1975 when he decided to give his time to his son and wife, which he continued to do until mid-1980 when he and Yoko Ono recorded *Double Fantasy*.

Paul McCartney was the most active of the group after their dissolution. He formed the group he called *Wings* and it turned out to be a highly successful supergroup of its own.

George and Ringo also pursued their own directions as musicians and turned out a number of hit records.

The following discography of recordings by the individual Beatles after they went their separate ways is presented to give an accurate portrait of the extent to which John, Paul, George, and Ringo went in their recording efforts as individuals.

* * *

JOHN LENNON

John's first three albums as a solo artist have since been deleted from Capitol Records' catalogue. They include: **Unfinished Music No. 2: Life With The Lions** (Capitol: *ST-3357*), which was released in May 1969; **Wedding Album** (Capitol: *SMAX-3361*) from October 1969; and **The Plastic Ono Band Live Peace In Toronto** (Capitol: *SW-3362*), issued in December 1969.

Plastic Ono Band (Capitol: *SW-3372*) arrived in

December 1970. It included these cuts: *Mother; Hold On; I Found Out; Isolation; My Mummy's Dead; Working Class Hero; Love; Remember; Well, Well, Well; God;* and *Look At Me.*

September 1971 saw the release of **Imagine** *(Capitol: SW-3379).* It featured these cuts: *Imagine; Crippled Inside; Jealous Guy; It's So Hard; I Don't Want To Be A Soldier; Oh My Love; Give Me Some Truth; How Do You Sleep; How;* and *Oh, Yoko.*

Mind Games *(Capitol: SW-3414)* was released in October 1973. The cuts on this album were: *Mind Games; Tight As; Aisumasen; One Day; Bring On The Lucie; Nutopian International Anthem; Intuition; Out On The Blue; I Know; Only People; You Are Here;* and *Meat City.*

Walls And Bridges *(Capitol: SW-3416)* was issued in September 1974. This LP's cuts were: *Going Down On Love; Whatever Gets You Thru The Night; Old Dirt Road; What You Got; Bless You; Scared; No. 9 Dream; Surprise, Surprise; Steel And Glass; Beef Jerky; Nobody Loves You;* and *Ya Ya.*

In February 1975 John's album **Rock'n'Roll** *(Capitol: SK-3419)* was released. The cuts included: *Be-Bop-A-Lula; Stand By Me; You Can't Catch Me; Ain't That A Shame; Do You Want To Dance; Sweet Little Sixteen; Slippin' & Slidin'; Peggy Sue; Bring It On Home To Me; Send Me Some Lovin'; Bony Moronie; Ya, Ya;* and *Just Because.*

Shaved Fish *(Capitol: SW-3421)* was released in October 1975. Its cuts included: *Give Peace A Chance; Mind Games; Imagine; Instant Karma; Whatever Gets You Through The Night; No. 9 Dream; Cold Turkey; Happy Xmas; Power To The People; Mother;* and *Woman Is The Nigger Of The World.*

Double Fantasy *(Geffen Records, manufactured exclusively by Warner Bros. Records Inc.)* released in November, 1980. Contains fourteen songs. For the first time, John Lennon's wife, Yoko Ono, sings with him. The cuts were: *(Just Like) Starting Over; Every Man Has A Woman; Cleanup Time; Give Me Something; I'm Losing You; I'm Moving On; A Beautiful Boy (Darling Boy); Matching The Wheels; I'm Your Angel; Dear Yoko; Beautiful Boys; Kiss, Kiss, Kiss; Woman; Hard Times Are Over.*

The album has a significant message from John and Yoko:

"With special thanks to all the people, known and unknown, who helped us stay in America, without whom this album would not have been made."

New York *Daily News* music critic Roy Trakin made this incisive observation about John Lennon's last record album:

"It is, of course, impossible to listen to John's homilies about love and family now without feeling the remorse of his senseless death. The man who was never afraid to share his fears and foibles with the rest of us finally seemed happy and fulfilled—and who are we to begrudge him that? There is another album of material awaiting release, some of it apparently more experimental. But listening to "Double Fantasy," one begins to realize that John was starting to rely on Yoko—and their home life— even more. Many people told John that Yoko's material was the best stuff on the record, and the fact that she was about to get that recognition as an artist made him look to the future with all the more enthusiasm."

* * *

PAUL McCARTNEY

McCARTNEY (Capitol: SMAS-3363) was Paul's first solo album, released in April 1970. Its cuts include: *Lovely Linda; That Would Be Something, OO You; Valentine Day; Every Night; Hot As Sunglasses; Junk; Man We Was Lonely; Momma Miss America; Teddy*

Boy; Singalong Junk; Maybe I'm Amazed; and *Kreen-Akrore.*

Paul's second solo album was *RAM (Capitol: SMAS-3375),* released in May 1971, and featuring his wife, Linda. Including are these cuts: *Too Many People; Three Legs; Ram On; Dear Boy; Uncle Albert/Admiral Halsey; Smile Away; Heart Of The Country; Monkberry Moon Delight; Eat At Home; Long Haired Lady;* and *Back Seat Of My Car.*

In December 1971, *Wings Wild Life (Capitol: SMAL-3386)* appeared. Its cuts were: *Wild Life; Mumgo; Big Bop; Love Is Strange; Some People Never Know; I Am Your Singer; Tomorrow;* and *Dear Friend.*

Red Rose Speedway (Capitol: SMAL-3409) was released in April 1973. The cuts on this LP were: *Big Barn Red; My Love; Get On The Right Thing; One More Kiss; Little Lamb Dragonfly; Single Pigeon; When The Night; Loup; Hold Me Tight; Lazy Dynamite; Hands Of Love;* and *Power Cut.*

November 1973 saw the release of *Band On The Run (Capitol: SO-3415).* Its cuts included: *Band On The Run; Jet; Bluebird; Let Me Roll It; Mrs. Vandebilt; Mamunia; No Words; Helen Wheels; Picasso's Last Words;* and *Nineteen Hundred & Eighty Five.*

Venus and Mars (Capitol: SMAS-11419) was released in June 1975. The album's cuts were: *Venus and Mars; Rock Show; Medicine Jar; You Gave Me The Answer; Letting Go; Love In Song; Magneto and Titanium Man; Call Me Back Again; Spirits Of Ancient Egypt; Treat Her Gently; Lonely Old People; Crossroads Theme;* and *Listen To What The Man said.*

In March 1976 *Wings At The Speed Of Sound (Capitol: SW-11525)* was released. Its cuts were: *Let 'Em In; Note You Never Wrote; She's My Baby; Beware My Love; Wino Junko; Silly Love Songs; Cook Of The House; Time To Hide; Must Do Something About It; San Ferry Anne;* and *Warm and Beautiful.*

December 1976 saw the arrival of *Wings Over America* *(Capitol: SWCO-11593)*. The three record LP included these cuts: *Venus And Mars/Rock Show/Jet; Let Me Roll It; Spirits Of Ancient Egypt; Medicine Jar; Maybe I'm Amazed; Call Me Back Again; Lady Madonna; The Long And Winding Road; Live And Let Die; Picasso's Last Words (Drink To Me); Richard Cory; Bluebird; Yesterday; You Gave Me The Answer; Magneto And Titanium Man; Go Now; My Love; Listen To What The Man Said; Let 'Em In; Time To Hide; Silly Love Songs; Beware My Love; Letting Go; Band On The Run; Hi, Hi, Hi; Solly, I've Just Seen A Face;* and *Blackbird*.

* * *

GEORGE HARRISON

George's first two record LPs as a solo artist have since been deleted from the Capitol catalogue. They are *WONDERWALL (Capitol: ST-3350)*, which was released in December 1968; and *ELECTRONIC SOUND (Capitol: ST-3358)*, issued in May 1969.

ALL THINGS MUST PASS (Capitol: STCH-639) came out in December 1970. Included on this three-record album were these cuts: *My Sweet Lord; Isn't It A Pity; All Things Must Pass; I'd Have You Anytime; Wah-Wah; What Is Life; If Not For You; Behind That Locked Door; Let It Down; Run Of The Mill; Beware Of Darkness; Apple Scruffs; Ballad Of Sir Frankie Crisp; Awaiting On You All; Art Of Dying; I Dig Love; Hear Me Lord; Out Of The Blue; Plug Me In; I Remember Jeep; Thanks For The Pepperoni;* and *Congratulations*.

George's *CONCERT FOR BANGLA DESH (Capitol: STCX-3385)* was released in December 1971. It featured a variety of recording artists who had appeared with George at the Madison Square Garden benefit concert in New York City. Included were these cuts and artists: *Bangla Dhun* (Ravi Shankar/Ali Akbar Khan/Alla Raka); *Wah-Wah; My Sweet Lord; Here Comes The Sun; Awaiting On You All; Bangla Desh; Something* (all by George Harrison); *That's The Way God Planned It* (Billy Preston); *It Don't Come Easy* (Ringo Starr); *Beware of Darkness* (George Harrison/Leon Russell); *While My Guitar Gently Weeps* (George Harrison/Eric Clapton); *Jumpin' Jack Flash* (Leon Russell); *Youngblood* (Leon Russell/Don Preston); *Hard Rain's Gonna Fall; It Takes A Lot To Laugh, It Takes A Train To Cry; Blowin' In The Wind; Mr. Tambourine Man;* and *Just Like A Woman* (all by Bob Dylan). A 64-page book was included as part of the record package.

May 1973 saw the release of *LIVING IN THE MATERIAL WORLD (Capitol: SMAS-3410).* Its cuts were: *Living In The Material World; Give Me Love; Sue Me, Sue You Blues; Light That Has Lighted The World; Don't Let Me Wait Too Long; Who Can See It; Lord Loves The One; Be Here Now; Try Some, Buy Some; Day The World Gets 'Round;* and *That Is All.*

DARK HORSE (Capitol: SMAS-3418) arrived in December 1974. Cuts on this LP were: *Dark Horse; Hari's On Tour; Simply Shady; So Sad; Bye Bye Love; Maya Love; Ding Dong, Ding Dong; Far East Man,* and *It Is.*

September 1975 marked the release of *EXTRA TEXTURE (READ ALL ABOUT IT) (Capitol: SW-3420).* On this album these cuts appeared: *You; Answer's At The End; This Guitar; Ooh Baby; World Of Stone; Bit More of You; His Name Is Legs; Can't Stop Thinking About You; Tired Of Midnight Blue;* and *Grey Cloudy Lies.*

In October 1976 *THE BEST OF GEORGE HARRISON (Capitol: ST-11578)* was released. Its cuts were: *Something; If I Needed Someone; Taxman; Here*

Comes The Sun; Think For Yourself; For You Blue; While My Guitar Gently Weeps; My Sweet Lord; Give Me Love; You; Bangla Desh; Dark Horse; and *What Is Life.*

George's most recent album is **THIRTY-THREE & 1/3 (Dark Horse: DH-3005)** and was released in November 1976. Its cuts include. *Woman Don't You Cry For Me; Dear One; Beautiful Girl; This Song; See Yourself; It's What You Value; True Love; Pure Smoky; Crackerbox Palace;* and *Learning How To Love You.*

* * *

RINGO STARR

Ringo's first album as a solo artist was **SENTIMENTAL JOURNEY (Capitol: SW-3365)**, released in May 1970. On it were these cuts: *Sentimental Journey; Night And Day; Bye Bye Blackbird; Whispering Grass; I'm A Fool To Care; Star Dust; Blue, Turning Grey Over You; Love Is A Many-Splendored Thing; You Always Hurt The One You Love; Dream; Have I Told You Lately That I Love You;* and *Let The Rest Of The World Go By.*

September 1970 saw the release of Ringo's second solo LP, **BEAUCOUPS OF BLUE (Capitol: SMAS-3368)**. It included these cuts: *Beaucoups Of Blues; Love Don't Last Long; Fastest Growing Heartache In The West; I'd Be Talking All The Time; Without Her; Wine, Women And Loud Happy Songs; Woman Of The Night; Fifteen Dollar Draw; I Wouldn't Have You Any Other Way; Loser's Lounge; Silent Homecoming;* and *Waiting.*

RINGO (Capitol: SWAL-3413) arrived in October 1973. The album's cuts were: *I'm The Greatest, Photograph; Six O'clock; Sunshine Life For Me; Oh My My; You're Sixteen; Step Lightly; You And Me; Devil Woman;* and *Have You Seen My Baby.*

In November 1974 *GOODNIGHT VIENNA (Capitol: SW-3417)* was released. Its cuts included: *It's All Down To Goodnight Vienna; Oo-Wee; Occapella; Husbands And Wives; Snookeroo; All By Myself; Call Me; No No Song; Only You;* and *Easy For Me.*

BLAST FROM YOUR PAST (Capitol: SW-3422) arrived in November 1975. This LP's cuts were: *You're Sixteen; No No Song; It Don't Come Easy; Photograph; Back Off Boogaloo; Only You; Beaucoups of Blues; Oh My My; I'm The Greatest;* and *Early 1970.*

Ringo's first album for Atlantic Records was *RINGO'S ROTOGRAVURE (Atlantic: SD-18193)* was released in September 1976. Its cuts were: *A Dose Of Rock 'n' Roll; Hey Baby; Pure Gold* (by Paul McCartney); *Cryin; You Don't Know Me At All; Cookin' (In The Kitchen Of Love)* (by John Lennon); *I'll Still Love You* (by George Harrison); *This Be Called A Song; Las Brisas; Lady Gaye;* and *Spooky Weirdness.*

A second album, *RINGO THE 4th (Atlantic: SD-19108),* was released by Atlantic in November 1977. Its cuts included: *Gave It All Up; Wings; Out On The Streets; Drowning In The Sea Of Love; Sneaking Sally Through The Alley; Simple Love Song; Tango All Night; Can She Do It Like She Dances; It's No Secret;* and *Gypsies In Flight.*

XIV

THE FIFTH BEATLE

Of all disc jockeys in the United States, Murray Kaufman—better known as Murray The K—was the one most closely and most intimately associated with The Beatles. His friendship and working relationship with John, Paul, George, and Ringo ranges back to their early days in New York when Murray The K was also Mr. Radio.

Teenagers in the late 1950s and early 1960s preferred Murray The K and The Swingin' Soiree on WINS in New York more than any other radio personality. When The Beatles invaded Manhattan in 1964, Murray The K became their friend and companion. He traveled with the group to other parts of the country, spent time with them in England, and got to know some of their friends, like The Rolling Stones.

As a result of that association, Murray The K became known as "The Fifth Beatle." More recently, Murray The K has been promoting the stage show *Beatlemania*.

Author Martin Grove, again in pursuit of intimate, inside information and color, as well as opinion, cornered Murray The K for an in-depth interview that followed this give and take:

Q. When did you first become aware that there was a group called the Beatles?

A. In October of '63. They brought a record to me, and mentioned the possibility that The Beatles might come to the U.S. I said, "Okay, I heard a lot about it." I put it on the air. I had a record review board contest on WINS at the time where I'd play five new records each day. The audience would vote on which record the liked best, and the winners of each week would be played on Saturday. When I ran them, (The Beatles) in a contest with a record called *She Loves You* it came in third out of the five records. But I still continued to play it for two or two-and-a-half weeks. Nothing happened. I mean, really no reaction. *Nothing!* During those days I was doing all the holiday shows at the Brooklyn Fox Theater. Ten days, six shows a day. The Christmas show came along. I did the show, and then decided to go to Florida for my vacation. While I was in Florida from nothing at all suddenly every time you put on the radio ever other record was *I Want To Hold Your Hand.* I remember saying, "Gee, that's the same group, only on this record sound like an English version of the Everly Brothers." It was that kind of sound. While I was there I received an urgent call from my station manager in New York at WINS. He told me that The Beatles are coming.

Q. How did you react to the news?

A. I said, "Fine. Get an exterminator." He said, "You don't understand, man. All the television people and newspaper people and radio people are going to be out covering their arrival. We're going to be the only radio station to cover it live. We want you back here."

Q. Did you jump at the chance?

A. I said, "Oh, forget it. I don't know them. They don't know me. I'm in the midst of a vacation I really need." Well, he really put the pressure on and forced me to return. We hopped on a plane and I came back to New York and went out there. I really wasn't too anxious for this whole deal. I walked into Kennedy Airport. Of course, in those days it was pretty much my town. The cops got me right into the press room where my engineer was. They had the radio people set up in the front, and the newspaper reporters were behind us. The cameramen were in the back. Then The Beatles walked in. We were doing it live. All of a sudden George Harrison turned to me and said, "I love your hat." I said, "You can have it." I also told him, "By the way, you came over on the plane with some friends of mine."

Q. Who were they?

A. At that time a group that was known as Murray The K's Dancing Girls had just cut their first record, *Be My Baby*. The girls, known as the Ronnettes, had been on the plane with Phil Spector, their producer. I mentioned this to George and he said, "Who are you?" I said, "I'm Murray The K." He asked, "You're Murray The K?" It seems that they had heard about me because all the acts that played The Brooklyn Fox Theatre would tell them about my shows when they went to England, and would play my albums for them. They all stopped with the news conference and started rapping with me to the dismay of the rest of the press corps.

Q. What did that lead to?

A. They said, "Hey, come on over to the Plaza. We want to talk to you." I said, "Okay, great." So I went over to the Plaza Hotel after I came back from Kennedy, and we had done this exclusive interview. While this whole conversation was going on we had scooped everybody else. I came back to WINS and everybody was saying, "Great! Great!" And I said, "Listen, I'm going over to their hotel. They asked me to come over. I don't know what's going to happen." WINS said, "Do anything you want." So I did. I walked over. There were 10,000 kids out front. I got up to the floor where The Beatles were. There must have been about 20 security guards there, I saw people there from other stations, really heavy news people and disc jockeys, trying to get in to see them. I walked up to the desk, and I knew this was going to be a hassle. I was just going to forget it. I was just going to leave my name, and let them know I had been there. I was going to split. I said, "Listen, I'm Murray The K..." Before I could get anything else out, they answered, "Oh, yeah. They're expecting you. Go right in." So I went in and that's when it all began.

Q. What a stroke of good luck!

A. It ended up that night that I did my radio show

from their hotel room. I wound up taking them out afterwards for dinner, and that kind of stuff. We got kind of friendly. Then I found out that it was going to snow the next day. They were supposed to take off for their first concert in the U.S., which was in Washington, D.C. So I told Brian Epstein he'd better hire a train. I told him to make arrangements to get a special train to get to Washington because they weren't going to be able to fly out of New York tomorrow. It was really going to be a heavy snowstorm.

Q. Did it actually snow?

A. Yes. It did snow. We went down to Washington, and had a lot of fun on the train. We almost got killed when we got off the train. Some 10,000 kids broke through the barriers. I remember being pinned against a locomotive on the outside, and feeling the life going out of me, and saying to myself, "My God. MURRAY THE K DIES WITH ENGLISH GROUP!" I wondered what my epitaph would be. George Harrison looked at me and said, "Isn't this fun?" I did my show that night right from their dressing room in Washington, D.C. We were talking and doing my radio show from there. We broadcast the concert, and then we came back to New York on the train. Then they had the *Ed Sullivan Show* to do. I stayed in their hotel suite and watched it. When they came back they invited me to come to Miami. But there were no hotel rooms available.

Q. How did you handle that crisis?

A. Cynthia Lennon was traveling with them. She was married to John at that time. Paul was sharing a room with Ringo. George said, "Hey, why don't you room with me?" So I did. I roomed with George while we were in Miami, and I did my radio shows right from their rooms. Then, because the press was on them all the time, I found them a place, a friend of mine's home, where they could go swimming and relax. I also knew somebody who had a big 90 foot yacht. We went out on that, and we just had a good old time trying to beat the press. They wanted to see some of the action there, so I took them to see The Coasters. They'd rather see The Coasters than, say, Sammy Davis Jr. They really wanted to see some of the rock acts.

Q. What happened after you returned to New York and The Beatles flew home to England?

A. Then came a lot of transatlantic telephone conversations and interviews over the phone—like the day the Sunday papers all carried stories saying that Paul had married Jane Asher. Everybody was calling me and complaining, "Murray, you didn't tell us." I said, "I don't think they are." I called Brian Epstein and he said, "It's ridiculous." He told me, "We're not going to speak to the press, but you can tell them that we're going to call you on the air tonight." And they did. Paul got on the phone and said it was a lie. Did a whole thing about it. He really put down the press for saying it. Then they invited me to England. I went, and they really built me up over there. They had me on every show, and then I introduced them at the *New Musical Express* Awards. That's where I met The Rolling Stones. John asked me if I'd bring The Stones over to the U.S., which I did a few months later.

Q. Obviously, then, you were one of the very first people in the United States to get to know the Beatles.

A. Right.

Q. What were they like back then when they were just starting out?

A. They blew everybody's mind away in the sense that they did not in any way, shape or form react like superstars had always reacted before. They put the press on. They really won everybody over with that. They looked upon the crowds as the crowds being the show and they the audience. They didn't take themselves seriously as superstars. They were just very much themselves and into having fun and finding out what was going on. They were very natural. Very together. Very disciplined. Very dedicated to wanting to sound good and make a good impression.

Q. What were they like as individuals? Who, for example, would you say was the most forceful member or the most dominant member of The Beatles then?

A. Well, people talked a great deal about that. There really was no dominant member. They really talked everything out. Brian would do something and they would talk it over as a group. The most inquisitive member, the person who would ask the most explicit questions, was George. He always wanted the answers and *why*. He was very direct. John, of course, was the most cynical and at the same time very friendly, Paul was a perfectionist, very cool and very much together. Ringo was very easy going. But there didn't seem to be any strong dominance by any one of them at that time. The dominance would take place, perhaps, or come on later in Paul being such a perfectionist in the studio. He was very heavily dedicated to that kind of thing. And they all started to become quite perfectionists. But Paul, in the studio, I would say was dominant. John, I guess, was the most vociferous, saying things or getting things together. He was a little older at the time. But there wasn't a very heavy dominance by one of them like people sometimes think.

Q. Was Ringo well integrated into the group at that point?

A. Oh, yeah.

Q. Despite the fact that he had come in as the last member, and was the new boy so to speak?

A. It was just like he had been with them for years. He just fit right in.

Q. How did The Beatles react to America on their first visit?

A. They didn't see much of it. They saw some of it, of course. In New York we went to the *Playboy Club*, I think, that first night for dinner. The press followed us and I remember them asking Paul, "What do you think of the *Playboy* bunnies? What do you think of *Playboy?*" And he said, "Well, you can write that *Playboy* and The Beatles are just good friends." That's the kind of thing. And someone would come over from, say, Idaho and say to one of them, "Here, boy, sign this." And they would do lines like, "Oh, sure, anything for an American. Don't you think so, Ringo? —Oh, yeah. That's it!"

Q. How did you get the nickname The Fifth Beatle?

A. It was in Washington. I think it was Ringo who did it. One guy asked him them some question, and they gave him a real typical Beatlesque kind of answer. They were really putting the press on. One reporter said, "Who's this fellow we see with you all the time?" They answered, "Oh, don't you know him? My goodness man. That's the Fifth Beatle."

That's where that was picked up. I was tagged with it after that. Then the station heard about it and started billing me on the air as The Fifth Beatle. I really didn't like it very much, but that was it.

Q. So The Beatles came to America and their records took off.

A. Yeah. They had ten on the charts at the same time. Anything they put out became a hit.

Q. Why do you think that was? What was it about The Beatles that sparked the imagination of so many fans?

A. My observance has been that every time we have a new musical phenomenon or a new superstar who comes along, it's always preceded by a national preoccupation with something or a national catastrophe. The Beatles were fulfilling what had happened in contemporary music for the past fifty years. We had a new superstar every nine years—in 1936 Benny Goodman, and the national preoccupation was coming out of the Depression; nine years after that, in '45, when we had more babies born in this country than at any other time, Frank Sinatra emerged and started the era of the vocalist at the end of World War II; Elvis Presley in '54 followed the Army-McCarthy Hearings. By that time everybody had a television set. The kids were really seeing their parents and their music and movies and rejecting it all. They wanted their own music—by teenagers for teenagers with Presley. Then nine years after that came The Beatles, which was preceeded by another national catastrophe, the assassination of President Kennedy. So looking for a new dimension and a new thing, along came four guys with a completely different attitude, who looked differently and spoke differently. It was the right time and the right place with the right people. Their attitude was right, as much at the beginning, even more so, than their music. You couldn't hear them except on records. I think that was the reason for their success. Of course, we've now gone so many years and we haven't had anybody come along to start a new musical era since The Beatles. So they still are that powerful. The time came when it was supposed to happen. We had Watergate and Viet Nam. But that's nothing to sing about!

Q. No, it's not. Murray, let me ask you to comment about how The Beatles changed as their time in the spotlight lengthened.

A. Well, it's like anything else. They changed. The thing that made them so powerful was that while most groups would continue to play—like Benny Goodman stayed Benny Goodman; Frank Sinatra stayed Frank Sinatra; Presley to the end stayed Presley—The Beatles changed with every album. A 180 degree change. With this instant change they also had reached a point where when they were on tour they were always together, just the four of them in their hotel room having to play it cool and watch whatever they did. Finally, they started to take separate vacations. I think that was in '65. That's when George found the Maharishi in India, and Paul went to Greece. What happened was that they started to become individuals as opposed to young kids with a group. They found women they loved. The separation from each other and their own individual lives began. Then the death of Brian Epstein made a tremendous contribution to their breaking up and having problems with Apple.

Q. Suppose Brian had not died at so young an age. Would things have gone differently for The Beatles?

A. I think the script would have read much differently than the way it eventually ended up for them.

Q. Do you believe it was inevitable that they would break up.

A. Yes. It was inevitable the way things were going. I mean, John and Paul started to have different ideas about writing. George wasn't too happy because he wasn't getting too many records on the albums.

Q. What are they like today? Do you see them now?

A. I saw Ringo and George most recently. George says he's happier now than he's ever been in his life. He's got all his stuff together.

Q. Is he living in New York or Los Angelese these days?

A. George has a place out here (in L.A.). He still has an estate in London, too. And Ringo's out here in Hollywood.

Q. What about John and Paul?

A. John lives on West 72nd Street in New York. He's got a co-op apartment there. Paul's places are in England and Scotland.

Q. We've heard so much talk about whether The Beatles will ever get together again. The question has come up as to whether they would do it for some astronomical amount of money, say $50 million?

A. No.

Q. You don't think they would?

A. No. Paul is a perfectionist. He worked very hard on Wings. It's what he wants to do and it's his music. They all say that, man, they'd have to get together and spend or six months just playing together to get it all together again.

You've got a dichotomy with their wives going now. You've got George into where his head is. They're just not together any more. It's over.

Q. And yet there seems to be an enormous market today for The Beatles. Capitol Records, of course, is reissuing their albums.

A. And our show, *Beatlmania,* is a big smash in New York.

Q. Tell me about Beatlmania. I know that you're coming to Los Angeles for at least 19 weeks at the Shubert Theatre, which says something right away!

A. It's an absolute smash in New York. Standing room only. A standing ovation at every performance!

Q. Is Los Angeles the second company to be opened?

A. Yes. But we're bringing the original cast in from New York.

Q. Are there plans to go out with a national company, too?

A. Yes. We will eventually go on tour. And we'll also go to Europe and to the Far East as well.

Q. There are several motion pictures in the works right now, too, dealing with aspects of The Beatles. Robert Stigwood is finishing Sgt. Pepper's Lonely Hearts Club Band in New York, with Peter Frampton and The Bee Gees starring.

A. Yes. And there's *I Want To Hold Your Hand* at Universal. I'm going to be in that picture.

Q. From what I've heard, that sounds like an interesting project.

A. It's about The Beatles' first week in New York.

Q. Why do you think that today's youngsters—many of whom weren't even in school in 1964—have such a strong interest in The Beatles?

A. Well, two reasons. First, the albums and the music they hear. They always have that. They've seen them in at least three motion pictures. And they hear The Beatles talk about them. And there's Paul McCartney and Wings and the George Harrison stuff. They've heard so much about The Beatles. And secondly, there never was another superstar to come along that they claim as their own. So they find the same excitement that their older brothers and sisters did in the '60s.

Q. Are The Beatles aware of the extent of all this continuing interest about them? How do they feel about it?

A. Oh, The Beatles feel that they don't want to get together.

Q. Do you think they are surprised that the public is still so hung up on them?

A. No.

Q. And you don't think anything would ever really bring them to the point of reuniting?

A. No, I don't think so.

Q. Where do they go from here?

A. Their own separate ways. They have their own lives. They'll follow their own paths.

Q. I've heard talk about the possibility that while all four of them might not get together we might someday see Ringo and George, for instance, team up to do something.

A. Oh, they're always doing something. Two or three of them always get into a studio and fool around a little bit. But never the four of them together.

Q. Have they ever released any of that material?

A. You mean, when they play on another person's record?

Q. Yes.

A. It's all been released. But they never mention that some of them are sitting in on it.

Q. That's very interesting, indeed.

A. Say Paul is in town and George is making a record. Paul may come in and play a couple of tunes. Or Ringo may sit in for one, you know. They do it. But they just do it as friends. Just getting together and having fun. But never the four of them together.

Q. So we may have heard the results of a Beatles reunion—or, at least, a semi-reunion without actually knowing it.

A. Yes. In a very masked different way.

BOOK III

LAST WORDS

XV

THE TRIBUTES—

A MIGHTY OUTPOURING

Fans and admirers around the world—from the high
est to the lowliest, from the White House and from 9
Downing Street to the dingy Liverpool backstreet where
John Lennon's dizzying climb to renown began, paid
tribute to the slain singer as perhaps no other entertainer
before him had been eulogized.

President Carter led the global outpouring of grief in
these words:

> "John Lennon helped create the music and
> mood of our time. His spirit, the spirit of the
> Beatles—brash and earnest, ironic and
> idealistic all at once—became the spirit of a
> whole generation.
>
> "His work as an artist and musician was far
> from done, but...he leaves an extraordinary
> and permanent legacy.
>
> "I know that I speak for many millions of
> Americans when I say that I am saddened by
> his death and distressed by the senseless
> manner of it. It is especially poignant that
> John Lennon has died by violence, though he
> had long campaigned for peace."

Former Prime Minister Harold Wilson, who
recommended the Beatles for the *Member Of The British
Empire* medal fifteen years previously, also had warm,
kind words for Lennon:

"He gave the kids something to think about. He kept
them off the streets and did more than all the forces of law

and order could have done put together."

New York Governor Hugh L. Carey said in a telegram to Yoko Ono:

"John Lennon was a man who stood for peace and non-violence and love and kindness...Your husband has been struck down under conditions that are tragic and are, frankly, sorrowful in our society."

Then the governor ordered flags on all public buildings in the state to be flown at half-staff in memory of the Beatle's death.

That act immediately precipitated an outpouring of outrage from a number of New York State veterans' groups.

Older vets objected to the memorial salute Carey ordered and the general sentiment expressed is best summarized in the statement by Leonard Baxter, state adjutant of the American Legion in Albany:

"We disagree and feel that a flag at half-staff is something that should be reserved for persons of real high stature. We don't have a stand on this particular person as an individual..."

Baxter said the Legion's position had no bearing on John Lennon's conviction for possessing drugs, his British citizenship, or the support he openly gave to antiwar activities during the Vietnamese conflict.

Joseph Gumo, state adjutant of the Veterans of Foreign Wars, stressed that, speaking only for himself and not the organization he heads, said:

"I feel sorry for his wife and kid, and I also think he was a hell of a singer. But I think Carey's decision to lower the flag to half-staff stinks."

He said a number of members of the VFW called him and said, in effect:

"It's crazy. It's unbelievable. The guy was not even an American citizen."

Robert Muller, executive director of the Vietnam Veterans of America, supported Carey:

"John Lennon was one of the great forces of good in the Vietnam era."

A spokesman for the Governor, Steve Morello, commented after the furor broke:

"We think it is appropriate for the state to honor the memory of people who have made a significant contribution in our State and to our State."

The Lord Mayor of Liverpool, James Ross, called for establishment of a music school for youngsters as a tribute to Lennon.

Elsewhere in the city of the Beatles' birth and the individual members' births, fans stood weeping and praying on Matthew Street, where the Beatles were discovered in the early 1960s playing to packed houses in the grim Cavern Club, long since a casualty of the wrecker's ball.

At the same time, John Chambers, head of the local Beatles' Fan club, said with tears in his eyes:

"It's bloody terrible, bloody terrible. What a shame to kill such a talent, such a fine, gentle human being."

Lennon's neighbor in the Dakota, conductor Leonard Bernstein, who said he always admired John's work, was so shaken he could only comment:

"We're all in a state of shock. His music will live as long as the music of Bach, Beethoven, or Brahms had lived."

From Lake Tahoe, where he was appearing in person, Sammy Davis eulogized:

"His loss is a real tragedy to the millions who loved him and his compositions."

Comedian Milton Berle, a Lennon fan though not from John's generation, said:

"I thought his musical compositions were giant-like in nature."

Paul McCartney:

"John was a great guy. He is going to be missed by the entire world. I can't take it in at the moment."

Pale and distraught at the news of Lennon's slaying,

McCartney, who had had differences with John in the past which helped lead to the breakup of *The Beatles*, said he was too shaken to say anything further.

George Harrison canceled a recording session scheduled for Tuesday and sent word he was too upset to say anything publicly.

Ringo Starr, flew to New York to console Yoko Ono. Before entering the Dakota, an associate said:

"Ringo is extremely shocked. He doesn't want to say anything."

Lennon's first wife Cynthia, now married for a third time and running a bistro in Wales, as Mrs. John Twist, stated:

"I would like to say how terribly upset we are at the sudden and tragic death of John.

"I have always had the deepest affection for John since the divorce and have always encouraged his relationship with Julian, (their 17-year-old son), which I thought was for the best.

Julian, of course, is particularly upset about it. It came so suddenly. Julian remained very close to his father in recent years and is hoping to follow a career in music.

"He was looking to his father for guidance. Julian was hoping to see his father shortly after Christmas. We don't know what will happen now."

Julian, who plays guitar and drums, and has hopes of following in his father's musical footsteps, left immediately for New York.

Staying with Cynthia after the tragedy was Maureen Cox, former wife of Ringo Starr. The two women have been close friends from their Beatles days.

Then tributes came from the fans, not those among the

high and the mighty, but the ones who shaped the hard core of Beatle fans and enabled the boys from Liverpool to become famous and wealthy beyond their wildest dreams.

A sampling of what they felt in their hearts and the thoughts running through their minds is presented here from the Letters-to the Editor column of the *New York Post,* whose circulation in the days following John Lennon's murder leapfrogged from an average daily figure of 700,000 as adverstised in the Page One logo, to well over a million and threatened to overtake the rival *Daily News,* America's largest circulation daily, with about 1,500,000.

Leonard Ginsberg of Brooklyn wrote:

The five people who reshaped America and who so drastically altered the consciousness of young people were all brutally murdered: John Kennedy, Bobby Kennedy, Martin Luther King, Allard Lowenstein; and now one of the greatest exponents of peace—John Lennon.

Some of the other letters read as follows:

John Lennon's death was a senseless, tragic waste. Once again, a gentle troubador poet falls victim to violence.

The only solace during this holy time of year is that Lennon's message of love and song will endure all the more until one day there truly will be peace on earth and good will to every citizen of our saddened planet.

NINO PANTANO
Brooklyn

The senseless murder of John Lennon is a loss for the whole world. He was a musical genius, who made the world a happier place for all of us and he will be greatly missed.

But his memory and music will be with us forever. Our

prayers to his wife Yoko and son Sean.

MICHALE FOGARTY
Berkley Heights, N.J.

The killing of John Lennon, brought about by a gun-toting lunatic, is enough to make one just give up. Isn't there someone who can at least begin to stop the horrible street violence, which is now obviously out of control?

The pleas of Yoko's brother, for her to come home to Japan, where she would not have to live in fear of guns, should be a searing message to us all.

R. POTENTE
Fair Lawn, N.J.

The greatest tribute we can pay to John Lennon is to work as arduously in the war against crime as we did against the war in Vietnam. Pray God, more songs will be written that promote non-violent behavior at home as well as between nations.

B.D.
Manhattan

Yesterday, the happiness of a warm guy made some little piggy a real nowhere man. Now a day in the life of a Beatles fan is all helter-skelter.

Tell me why it had to happen just when it felt like you were starting over.

ARTHUR FINLAY, JR.
The Bronx

It is both ironic and tragic that a man who spent so much of his musical talents working for peace and brotherhood should meet such a violent and utterly senseless death.

DAVID LEVIN
Queens

I extend my deepest condolences and prayers to Yoko Ono, along with a word of comfort: although death has taken John from your side, he will never leave your heart. Finally, John, thanks for everything.

TOM CUNNIFF
Bronx

When Mark Chapman pulled the trigger Monday night, he did more than just kill John Lennon, more than merely cause a life to end.

When Mark pulled the trigger, something in every one of us died along with John Lennon.

PHILIP GELLIS
Long Beach

John Lennon and Allward Lowenstein, two men who campaigned for peace and civil rights, were gunned down mercilessly in the prime of their lives.

It's ironic that both killers admired their victims.

IRVING MENCHIN
Brooklyn

In memory of John Lennon:
Shots in the night,
And you were gone.
You gave us so much,
And it's there in your songs.

BENTE BAIO
Brooklyn

It is now a time of intense sorrow, since the inevitable great shadow has been cast upon John Lennon, a man in the prime of his life.

JOHN WECK, JR.
Metuchen, N.J.

Wake up America, wake up New York. How many

other John Lennons must be killed before we realize the sad shape we are in.

Criminals have been idolized and now our idols are fallen.

MARY ANN PANTANO
Brooklyn

Nothing, even new laws will stop the wanton murders and vicious atrocities perpetrated against innocent people here in the city.

The death of John Lennon only serves to highlight the inability of our society to control its destiny.

R.O. WEIHL
Manhattan

With three friends, some 15 years ago, John Lennon changed music.

The joy that he brought to us through his music and art became a part of our lives.

Now it's all over because of some foolish person with a gun.

TIM HATCHER
Manhattan

The masses who gathered outside the Dakota on hearing of the death of John Lennon tesitifies to the greatness of the ex-Beatle.

Many, when interviewed, couldn't really explain why they came. They just felt they had to be there. I share their grief.

A. CHAMBERS
Brooklyn

XVI

COMMENTARY

Two days after John Lennon was gunned down in New York City, the front page news of this heinous assassination remained a Page One headline in only two of the metropolis' three daily newspapers.

The *Daily News*, America's largest circulation daily clarioned in its banner:

JOHN'S WILL:
$30M PLUS
Half to Yoko, rest to trust

The *New York Post*, the nation's fastest-growing newspaper and largest afternoon in America chronicled this Page One headline over an exclusive photo of the dead Beatle lying in the Campbell Funeral Home mortuary just before his cremation:

YOKO SHOWS
SON WHERE
DADDY LIES

The August *New York Times* displayed eight headlined stories on Page One plus two four-line "teasers" trumpeting news buried on inside pages. Among the stories on the first page were:

BREZHNEV URGES U.S.
TO AGREE TO A BAN
ON MEDDLING IN GULF

SENATE DROPS CURB
ON U.S. BUSING SUITS

FROM FINANCING BILL

New Cable Network Buys Rights
To BBC Shows, Long a PBS Stable

And finally, but by no means least:

Mrs. Harris Angered by
Testimony at Tarnower Trial

Under that headline about the trial of Jean S. Harris for the love-triangle murder of famed Scarsdale Diet Dr. Herman Tarnower, the *Times* ran a two-column sketch by artist Marilyn Church which was drawn in the courtroom, where no cameras were permitted, and which depicted, according to the caption, the once-classy schoolmarm "speaking angrily with James Reichler, one of her lawyers, following testimony by Detective Arthur Siciliano yesterday in White Plains."

To follow the story along the five inches of one-column type on Page One, you would have to turn to Page 13, Column 1, and read another 19-Î inches of one-column type to its conclusion.

Overall, space devoted to this story—counting more type, sketch and headlines on the saga of a woman who allegedly shot to death a doctor over his love for another woman—totalled thirty-nine column inches.

The motto of the *Times* is:

"All the News
That's Fit to Print"

That logo has appeared in the "ear"—a box on the left top of the front page—for more years than any of us alive today can remember.

To follow what was going on in the aftermath of John Lennon's brutal, tragic murder on Day 3, a *Times* reader would have to scour the *Index,* a three-column "road map" to stories on the inside pages which always appears in the daily *Times* on the first place of its second, or "B," section.

Of the seventy stories *Times'* editors selected to showcase for their readers under such categories as "International," "Government/Politics," "General," Education/Welfare," "The Home Section," and seven other compartments into which news and features are slotted, the reference to a story or stories on John Lennon's death was listed fifth and last under the "General" heading and it read:

> Lennon murder suspect is
> "a different person" to father.......B3

Turning to page B3 on that Thursday morning, December 11, 1980, a *Times* reader would be greeted by a 10-inch-deep, five-column spread comprising a six-inch, three-column display of three photos—Mark David Chapman, the accused slayer; Julian Lennon, the 17-year-old-son of the murdered Beatle, and some members of a crowd of several hundred mourners at a vigil, now nearly three days old, outside the Dakota apartments, on Manhattan's Central Park West, where Lennon was suddenly and without warning shot to death by five bullets fired from a .38-caliber pistol manufactured by the Charter Arms Corporation of Bridgeport, Connecticut.

There were two stories in that "spread" on Page B3. One headline trumpeted:

Lennon Murder Suspect
"Different Person" to Father

That story, written by Dudley Clendinen, bore on the news that Mark David Chapman's father, David Curtis

Chapman, had remained bivuoaced in his white frame-and-brick house in northeastern Atlanta, and was refusing to give interviews to reporters, camped for two days with cameramen, on the front lawn.

Chapman finally called police to disperse the newsmen, but then some hours later he spoke briefly with a reporter from the *Times,* presumably by phone, presumably to Clendinen, although the narrative did not mention the *how* and *why* elements that also must go into a news story beside the *who, what, when,* and *where* constituents.

That report ran 10 1/2 inches of type.

The other story, a two-column piece, was written by Paul Montgomery under the headline:

Suspect in Lennon's Slaying Is Put Under Suicide Watch

The story itself was told in 15 1/2 inches of type.

Therefore, the total amount of reading space devoted to John Lennon's death on the dawn of Day 3 A.D. was twenty-six inches—or thirteen column inches less than the thirty-nine devoted to a story, if not kinky then at the very least appealing to prurient interests. The public has been lapping up sex, vice, crime, and murder sagas since the halcyon days of "yellow journalism," but seldom in the annals of crime have there been the elements of unsavory bed-hopping and sexual relationships that the Jean Harris-Herman Tarnower opus has foisted on the reading public. This certainly wasn't a "family newspaper" story.

Even the *Daily News,* a tabloid trying now to shake its years-long image of screaming sensationalism, and the *New York Post,* now surpassing anything America's largest city has ever known in blood and guts journalism, were both relatively subdued in their coverage of that story which, in essence, was of local interest—despite the fact that it commanded early attention in the world press, mostly because Dr. Tarnower's diet book was on the paperback best-seller lists, as it still was during the trial, more than a year after the murder in the physician's Westchester County mansion.

The *News* devoted twenty-five inches of type to the proceedings in court the previous day and the *Post* gave it a typically huge two-line, five-column headline on Page 15 totalling twelve inches of space over only twelve inches of well-composed, all-telling prose by reporter Joe Nicholson.

These comparisons on the coverage given to news in the New York City area by three of America's largest circulation newspapers raises a number of critical questions. Not the least of these is what thinking went on in the editorial conferences at the *New York Times* when preparations were made for coverage of news and the makeup for the next day's newspaper.

It certainly seems that the *Times'* editors placed more impact on the Harris-Tarnower story than the follow-up news on John Lennon's death—a story at that very time and for days and weeks afterward still commanding headlinese in newspapers around the world.

John Lennon's murder was one of the biggest news stories of 1980, which by the evening of Monday, December 8th, was rapidly approaching a new year. No other story commanded more shock value since the senseless assassinations of Senator Robert F. Kennedy and the Rev. Martin Luther King and, before those, perhaps the most shocking murder of the century, the slaying of President John F. Kennedy.

No commentary on the death of John Lennon carried more sense nor poignancy than the editorial in the *New York Post* written by Editorial Page Editor Bruce Rothwell.

"For millions of people throughout the world John Lennon was so much more than a composer of genius of popular songs. He was the voice of the generation."

The editorial went on to point out that Lennon, together with the second most outstanding of the four Beatles, Paul McCartney, inspired the singing quartet and helped significantly in their great success.

They created a "social revolution," Rothwell wrote so correctly.

"They sang of teenage love and hope but they sang for all of us, the very young and the very old, even for the tired and the jaded and despairing, for they sang of diamonds in the sky and the millenium:

> *I'll tell you something*
> *I think you understand*
> *Then I'll say that something*
> *I want to hold your hand*

Had the editors of the *New York Times* heard these words ever?

Were they aware of the "social revolution" the Beatles created the moment the late TV host, the inimitable Ed Sullivan, introduced them on his Sunday night CBS network show a generation ago?

People by the thousands, perhaps the millions may or may not have lost weight following Dr. Tarnower's diet plan. But can anyone equate Dr. Tarnower's murder to John Lennon's cold-blooded, unprovoked killing?

All people are created equal, all people are entitled to live their lives to the fullest, and n o one has a right to take another's life. That phrase has been uttered in many other ways and in many other places. Beyond the concept of this basic truth lies the question of placing values on the life and death of Dr. Tarnower and upon the life and death of John Lennon.

The anger demonstrated in the courtroom by Mrs. Harris, amounted to telling one of her lawyers during a recess, "Shut up. If you say that ag ain, I'm..." The rest of the comment wasn't heard by reporters.

Does an outburst of that sort become "...News That's Fit to Print" on Page One while on-going public grief and continuing mourning over the death of John Lennon, as well as the turning of the wheels of justice for the accused killer as he goes from courtroom to psychiatric detention for mental tests, command only back-of-the-paper treatment?

Whose loss meant more to the world—Tarnower's or Lennon's?

"Their words and music were the sounds of freedom and it is the tragic irony of Lennon's death that he was felled by a devoted follower who had lost his way," wrote Rothwell in the *Post*. "It used to be that every generation had its own war: now, it seems its heroes are gunned down on the streets where they live."

The editorial went on to name the aforementioned martyrs—the Kennedy brothers, Dr. King, "now Lennon—all senselessly killed."

Was Tarnower's killing senseless? Certainly there are many who will agree that all killing is senseless. There may be some person who will say "the dirty rat got what he had coming" because he was sleeping with another woman while also bedding down with society's darling schoolmistress, Jean Harris. Many women will understand the hurt Mrs. Harris must have experienced that moment she stepped into Dr. Tarnower's master bedroom and found the other woman's clothes about the room.

Mrs. Harris was toting a .32-caliber revolver that she had bought a few days before in Virginia, where you don't have to do much explaining to authorities to warrant the issuance of a license to bear such a dangerous weapon.

It apparently was no more difficult to obtain a license in Hawaii for the .38-Charter Arms revolver that Mark David Chapman brought with him from Honolulu to New York on his mission to commit a murder most foul.

247

"It may well be that there is no protection anywhere or at any time from anyone with the rage to kill," wrote Rothwell. "But must we make it so easy for deranged minds to 'get a gun and bring it so far to be within close aim of their victims?"

Mrs. Harris travelled some 300 miles to Dr. Tarnower's home in Purchase and, in the bedroom where he had "no protection anywhere" he met death from the business end of a .32's barrel.

John Lennon's plight was similar in some respects. He had "no protection anywhere" when he was shot with five bullets from that Charter Arms .38 carried 6,000 miles to the scene of death.

In citing the monumental loopholes of the 1968 Gun Control Act, enacted by Congress after the Bobby Kennedy and Martin Luther King assassinations, Rothwell's *Post* editorial stressed that one of that law's commandments is that purchasers of pistols are required "to state in writing that they have no history of mental incompetence or a criminal record."

Then the writer asked:

"But what use is gun registration when there is no check on an applicant's record?"

Can it be a sign of the times, of a society which no longer has an ability to place values on mankind and its actions, that we find Mrs. Harris' dirty linen being aired on the public washline, and dignified with Page One treatment in the *Times,* while the whys and wherefores of John Lennon's recent murder are relegated to the back pages?

The newspaper's editors have much to explain for the seeming imbalance and incongruity in their treatment of the two stories on the dawn of Day 3 following that act of madness that ended John Lennon's journey of triumph over the forty short years of his life.

Making "Mrs. Harris Angered by Testimony at Tarnower Trial" more important news than John

Lennon's brutal, cold-blooded murder, may have made it a time, too, when the *New York Times* must reassess its own set of values and ponder anew precisely what constitutes "All the News That's Fit to Print."

The *New York Times* doesn't stand alone in apparent need of taking a second look at its policies in judging the value of news. The Columbia Broadcasting System shares a need for a reappraisal of its own set of values.

Syndicated columnist Mike Royko brought that need to the forefront after John Lennon's murder. Royko wrote:

"I was pleased to see that the stories reporting the death of John Lennon were specific and accurate about the kind of gun that was used to murder the world-renowned musician.

"It was a .38-caliber pistol made by Charter Arms Corp. of Bridgeport, Connecticut."

Royko asked what difference it made to identify the gun manufacturer, then he proceeded to say it made a big difference to Charter Arms Corp.

Seems that back in 1974 when Alabama ex-Governor George C. Wallace was paralyzed, the bullet in his spine had been fired from a Charter .38.

But that wasn't how a CBS reporter told it on network TV. He reported that Wallace was done in by a "cheap handgun," obviously an allusion to the "Saturday night special," a gun so dismally inaccurate that one cannot "hit the side of a barn"—and yet so dreadfully deadly that literally thousands of persons die each year from the bullets fired by those guns.

The idea that the reporter called a Charter .38 a "cheap handgun" infuriated the gun company's brass. To such an extent that they demanded an apology from CBS.

While some persons may find it hard to believe, others will say *believe*—because CBS actually did humble itself at the altar of Charter Arms Corporation.

Royko got his hands on a copy of the company's magazine, or "house organ" as legitimate journalists refer to these puff publications. The editorial headline in the magazine told it succinctly:

An Apology from CBS

The body of the editorial, quoted by Royko, read:

"We are too dedicated to high quality in American-made handguns, and have poured too much of ourselves into our products to have one of them even casually referred to as a 'cheap handgun'.

"That was exactly the phrase used in a broadcast description of the handgun used by Arthur Bremer in his assassination attempt of Gov. Wallace, which happened to be one of our Undercover .38 Specials.

"The broadcast emanated from CBS...and our public relations people were immediately instructed to bring the error to their attention."

If indeed CBS apologized, it speaks volumes about the power of the gun lobby. Not only is it, as everyone knows, deeply entrenched in the halls of Congress, but the tentacles of this all-potent force spread like the webs of a hoary spider to every state capital in these United States.

And now, with one of the nation's most respected news media yielding to such an inane and inappropriate demand by Charter, it comes time to ask just how much embarrassment the network apology heaped on such brave reporters and commentators as Walter Cronkite, Mike Wallace, Morley Safer, Dan Rather, Harry Reasoner and the many other correspondents who'd rather turn in their press cards than become apologists to a company that is, however indirectly and inculpably— yet nevertheless actually—mass producing every year weapons used in perhaps dozens, perhaps scores or even hundreds and thousands of crimes ranging from armed robbery to murder?

Columnist Royko went on to quote from the Charter publication editorial the correspondence dispatched by a contrite CBS official:

"I am sending a copy of your letter to all our TV producers. In the event that we make reference to the Undercover .38 Special used by Arthur Bremer, we will certainly avoid characterizing it as a 'Saturday Night Special' or any other term which labels it as a 'cheap weapon'."

Royko said he didn't know whether it was "mere coincidence" that both Wallace's assassin and John Lennon's accused slayer chose the weapon because they both recognized quality when they went to buy the Charter .38.

The columnist then suggested that Charter Arms, which could not claim its "quality" gun took the lives of the two Kennedys and Rev. King, because weapons from other manufacturers were used in those murders, was now in a position to trumpet the wonders of its weapon to the world. Or as Mike Royko put it:

"Now that Charter Arms Corp. has the unique distinction of having two famous people shot by one of their products, I wonder if they have considered using it in their advertising.

"Something simple and tasteful like: 'The .38 that got George Wallace and John Lennon. See it at your gun dealer now.' "

The word count was just enough to buy the $200 agate line advertising space at the bottom of the *New York Times'* Page One columns or, if the company chose to go into display advertising with that slogan, it could take out a sparkling full five-column ad for $2000—running alongside a full one-column story jump from Page One.

Times editors may have believed they were giving the Scarsdale murder case a touch of class by starting it on Page One and continuing it next to the full five-column ad on B13. This was a page with a five-column Lord &

Taylor display clarioning the department store's "American Christmas" and saying, "A shared tradition since 1826. Today at Lord & Taylor come discover our many ways to give Izod."

Izod is not in Volume 1, Part I of the Britannica World Language edition of Funk & Wagnalls Standard Dictionary, but it is a word that Lord & Taylor customers understand—it represents the little alligator that dresses up their classic cardigans and Lacoste cotton shirts.

It would be most inappropriate for Charter to ask that its Page One agate ad be placed under a column of the Harris-Tarnower story or alongside the jump page in a five-column display beside that story's rambling continuation of twenty-one more inches of type.

If form holds true and Charter insists on total accuracy in the media, then its advertisements should and must appear in tandem with accounts of John Lennon's murder and not Dr. Tarnower's. Because it must be made perfectly clear, for accuracy's sake, that Mrs. Harris pulled the trigger of a .32-caliber Harrington & Richardson revolver with a two-inch barrel, which no one should mistake for a "Saturday Night Special" or "cheap handgun" either.

The problem is not so much the slight or snub or inadequacy that the *New York Times* demonstrated in its coverage of John Lennon's murder as it did in the death of John Lennon, caused by a fusillade of bullets fired from a .38-cal. Charter Arms Undercover .38 Special—a gun sold over the counter in Honolulu, a city of the United States of American, and without so much as a questioned asked.

The problem is not so much the apologist stance that CBS-TV assumed when the flack from Charter Arms' flacks created such a stir at the network that its officials fell over each other to stink up the joint with their "so sorry" letter to the company that manufactured the guns that killed not only John Lennon and wounded Governor Wallace, but which killed, wounded, or at the very least scared half to death those lucky ones who looked down the barrel of Charter Arms weaponry but escaped the deadly lead those barrels spew.

The problem is the statistics of gunslaughter for the United States. It is now, and has been for many years, shocking the conscience of a nation— as well as a civilized world. For nowhere else on this planet is human life taken as readily and as frequently as in this country by guns such as those produced by Charter Arms and by Harrington & Richardson and by other so-called "quality" gun manufacturers, as well as by the discredited makers of the "Saturday Night Specials" and other "cheap handguns," the latter two being the designations so abhorred by Charter Arms.

The list of killings of famous people by gunfire is a shameful blemish on the history of the United States— Abraham Lincoln, James A. Garfield, William McKinley, John Fitzgerald Kennedy, Robert F. Kennedy, Martin Luther King, and now John Lennon.

"Each new outrage," voiced an editorial in the New York *Daily News,* "brings with it a renewed outcry for strict national gun control laws. And each time the gun lobbyists beat it back."

The newspaper then offered a suggestion which is seconded and adapted by the author, the editors, and publisher of this book dedicated to the memory of John Lennon:

"Perhaps the vast army of John Lennon's admirers— who number in the tens of millions and make up a true cross-section of America—will rally to the gun control cause now and make it a truly effective political force. Surely there could be no greater tribute that his followers could pay to this gentle, humane man."

The wording of the *News'* suggestion can be made just a bit stronger to read:

"The vast army of John Lennon's admirers...*must* rally to the gun control cause" etc.

Indeed those milions of fans *must* rally and inundate their local political leaders, state legislators, governors, congressmen, senators, and even the President of the United States, with their written pleas for strict, hard-hitting gun controls. They must become even more active than the powerful and insidious gun lobbies which persist with seemingly undiminished vigor and influence despite the awesome weight of so much blood of the dead that covers them.

The suggestion to appeal to the President for gun controls could be a futile effort. For in the aftermath of John Lennon's assassination, Reagan, then still President-elect, did not indicate any eagerness to legislate gun controls. In fact, he demonstrated just the opposite tendency.

"I believe," he said, "in the kind of handgun legislation we have in California."

The law in that state mandates the imposition of an additional three-year sentence to the term given to any defendant found guilty of a felony. However, statistics show that since the law went into force July 1, 1977, the percentage of murders committed with firearms has increased, the murder rate for every 100,000 population went up, and the number of murders has risen.

And don't count on Nancy Reagan exerting influence on her husband to go the other way either. Not when she tells the world that she sleeps with a little gun under her pillow when Ronnie's on the road.

Yet there could be no greater tribute from his fans than to try and make this world the one which John Lennon sang about so often....